Combating Exclusion

Lessons from the Third EU Poverty Programme in Ireland

Brian Harvey

© **1994**
Combat Poverty Agency, Dublin Travellers Education and Development Group (DTEDG),
Forum, PAUL Partnership,
Research and Development Unit, Ireland.

Published by
Combat Poverty Agency, Dublin Travellers Education and Development Group (DTEDG),
Forum, PAUL Partnership,
Research and Development Unit, Ireland.

ISBN 1 871643 34 1

Photography
DTEDG: Derek Speirs
Forum: Ena Coleman, Frank Dolan, Helmut Gerversman
PAUL Partnership: Billy Kelly, Kenneth Shanks, Eoin Stephenson

Design and Production
Language *visual communication*

Distributed by
Combat Poverty Agency, 8 Charlemont Street, Dublin 2
Tel. 01 478 3355

The views expressed in this report are not necessarily
those of the Combat Poverty Agency.

CONTENTS

Overview
Main conclusions and recommendations   v

Author's Preface   xv

Chapter 1
Unemployment, poverty and social exclusion in Ireland   1

Chapter 2
The Poverty 3 programme   5

Chapter 3
Dublin Travellers Education and Development Group (DTEDG)   15

Chapter 4
Employment, economic development and social exclusion   23

Chapter 5
Social welfare and social exclusion   39

Chapter 6
Education and social exclusion   45

Chapter 7
Forum   59

Chapter 8
Legal and civic rights and social exclusion   67

Chapter 9
Health, accommodation and social exclusion   77

Chapter 10
Local development and social exclusion   89

Chapter 11
PAUL Partnership   97

Chapter 12
Organisational responses to social exclusion   107

Chapter 13
Implications for policy and action   119

References and Bibliography   125

Main conclusions and recommendations

Introduction
The Programme
The Third EU Poverty Programme, known as Poverty 3, has been in operation since early 1990. In Ireland, with funding assistance from a statutory body, the Combat Poverty Agency (CPA), the programme co-financed three projects. The programme also funded a Research and Development Unit (RDU) which, with the cooperation of the CPA, provided the projects with technical assistance and other supports.

Poverty 3 has a number of distinct features. First, its understanding of poverty is not simply as a matter of being financially poor but as exclusion from the rights, benefits and opportunities that are taken as the norm in contemporary society. Significantly, the full title of the programme is 'Medium Term Community Action Programme to Foster the Social and Economic Integration of the Least Privileged Groups'.

Second, in the context of combating exclusion and fostering integration the central aims of Poverty 3 are to stimulate experimental action, to formulate novel measures and models of local organisation, and to demonstrate the relevance of the lessons learned for mainstream policies and administrative practices. It seeks to identify good practice, to encourage policy development and public debate on anti-poverty action.

Third, a requirement of the programme was that its implementation locally should be based on key principles, among which were: to undertake a comprehensive set of actions ranging across several sectors and coordinated through a coherent, area-based, integrated plan; to enable the least privileged groups to take part in decisions affecting them; and to establish structured partnerships so as to combine the efforts of a number of key players in combating exclusion.

The Projects
Two of the three Irish projects are area-based actions. Forum in north-west Connemara represents a disadvantaged rural area in a peripheral region. The PAUL (People Action against Unemployment Ltd.) Partnership in Limerick City typifies the problems of a deprived urban area of public authority housing and high unemployment. The third project, the Dublin Travellers Education and Development Group (DTEDG), is concerned with the social exclusion of Travellers as a specific minority group.

Reporting on the Programme

In March 1993 an interim account, *Combating Exclusion in Ireland: A Midway Report*, was published. In late 1993 Brian Harvey was commissioned by the Editorial Committee (itself a partnership of representatives of the RDU, the CPA and the Irish projects) to prepare a final stage report on the programme in Ireland.

Here the Editorial Committee summarises the main conclusions and recommendations contained in, or arising from, Brian Harvey's report. The following sections, in their sequence and headings, correspond with the ordering of the principal themes and chapters in the main report.

From poverty to social exclusion: implications of a concept

Earlier EU poverty programmes were a response to the 're-discovery of poverty'. But 'poverty' is a *static* and limiting concept; it leads to an emphasis on dealing with the immediate problems of the poor, and to a restricted set of measures for this purpose.

In adopting the broader concept of social exclusion - i.e., a failure in economic and social integration - Poverty 3 highlights the range of *dynamic* processes by which people become poor and remain poor. Poverty is created by the way policies in general are devised and implemented; by the way labour markets operate to deprive people of jobs; by deficiencies in the systems of delivering education, health and social welfare; by the denial of rights - legal, civic and cultural; by inadequate housing infrastructures and services; and by geographical isolation. Poverty also means being excluded from participation in decision-making structures.

The various chapters in the main report indicate the diversity of activity within the projects and reflect the multidimensional concept of exclusion which underpins the Poverty 3 programme.

'Combating social exclusion' is now firmly on the policy agendas of the European Union and the Irish Government (see e.g., the Agreement on Social Policy in the Maastricht Treaty, and Chapter 7 of the *National Development Plan 1994-99*). But the practical implications of this policy aspiration have yet to be fully understood by policymakers. Combating exclusion means addressing its causes more than dealing with its symptoms. It means that the actions required are not to be confined to one or two Government

Departments. And it means that multi-sectoral actions 'on the ground' have to be complementary and mutually supportive within a cohesive programme.

At local level this integrated approach demands that agencies actively collaborate through partnership structures. The projects in Poverty 3 show that partnerships can work but much effort, learning and understanding are necessary. However, area-based partnerships may exclude minority groups such as Travellers, unless their inclusion is explicitly considered.

Combating exclusion requires resources, especially from public funds which are always scarce, relative to the needs to be met. But the manner in which public funds are created and allocated is a function of the dominant values and ideologies in our society. Some change in these is necessary if actions to combat exclusion are to be adequately resourced.

The sections below show how the comprehensive concept of 'combating social exclusion' was translated into actions at project level.

Resource development and employment
With the support of Bord Iascaigh Mhara (Irish Sea Fisheries Board), Forum organised three cooperatives to develop shellfish farming for the benefit of low income people. Its experience in this regard shows that for local people to share in the potential wealth of aquaculture there must be (i) intensive technical support from statutory agencies, (ii) resources for local group organisation and capacity building, and (iii) appropriate financial packages such as low interest loans.

Similarly, Forum points out that in tourism development small-scale providers in rural areas can be excluded by the current emphasis on large-scale capital investments. It has proposed an alternative approach to local tourism development to correct this imbalance.

PAUL illustrates the problems and possibilities of helping people out of unemployment at the lower ends of the labour market. The project identified the inadequacies of the existing Social Employment Scheme as the principal labour market measure for the long-term unemployed. It also confirmed the need for a concerted package of improved incentives and technical supports to facilitate the start-up of small businesses. Other important strategies in improving job prospects are training, guidance and counselling, and positive discrimination in recruitment.

DTEDG shows that there exists a distinctive Traveller economy, a key component of which is waste recycling. The potential of this needs to be recognised by local authorities - in their planning and administration - and by a number of other policies affecting Travellers (e.g., in the social welfare and employment codes).

Social Welfare: policy and administration

Local projects have an important function in supplementing the work of the Department of Social Welfare and of Citizens Information Centres in reducing the complexities of the social welfare code, and in informing people of their rights and entitlements.

Following its work on household debt and a study of moneylending practices, PAUL recommends alternative systems of debt management and stricter legislation to control moneylending. It has also promoted access to low cost credit as an alternative to reliance on moneylenders in areas neglected by mainstream credit institutions.

For Travellers in Dublin the system of delivering social welfare benefits is discriminatory, in that the majority can only obtain their entitlements through one central office.

The unique practice of requiring Travellers in receipt of Social Welfare to 'sign on' at a specific time should be ended, as should the segregated system of centralised supplementary welfare payments for Travellers in Dublin.

Education

Deficits in the education system defined by Forum were: inadequate remedial services, the lack of a statutory youth service, and poor provision for adults.

In cooperation with the Department of Education, an Education Resource Centre was established to support the roles of local schools, teachers, other professionals (e.g., in speech therapy), and parents. A 'resource model' of education being developed by Forum is recommended for a sparsely populated region of small and dispersed schools.

Research by PAUL highlighted the hidden costs of 'free' education for low-income families, and people's lack of awareness of the available support schemes. There is need to minimise the complexity of procedures used to assess eligibility for a range of schemes in which the applicants and levels of entitlement are quite similar.

On the basis of an early intervention programme targeted to the junior cycle at primary school, PAUL clarified the reforms required in the curriculum, in teaching practices, and in home/school links so as to work towards addressing educational failure among low income households. Meanwhile, PAUL's work in promoting access for adult tutors and learners to accredited educational opportunities charts an important new step in the expanding adult and community education sector.

Travellers are one of the groups most excluded from the education system, being virtually absent from second and third level. However, in order to make long-term progress, priority needs to be given to pre-school and primary level provision. This calls for an intercultural curriculum - to take account of Traveller culture - with appropriate teacher training, syllabi and teaching materials.

Failure to invest adequately at the primary level for all least privileged groups simply stores up problems of exclusion which must be addressed in later life.

Political, legal and civic rights

Fundamentally, combating exclusion is a matter of extending and guaranteeing citizens' rights.

Travellers experience particular forms of exclusion which is manifested in widespread negative attitudes and stereotyping, combined with prejudicial perceptions which ascribe to the travelling people a socially inferior and problem status.

A core value of DTEDG - which underlies all its policy proposals - is that Travellers are a distinct ethnic group whose culture, including nomadism, must be respected. This means that Travellers should retain their own group identity rather than be assimilated with the settled population.

Much of the work of the Travellers' project has been concerned with changing the way travelling people are perceived at official level and among the public. The project thus recommends that due consideration must be given to the distinctiveness of Traveller culture and identity, reinforced by a framework of civic and legal rights.

A solid legal basis is required to end discrimination against Travellers in daily life and commerce, and to set standards for public administration and popular attitudes.

Health, housing and accomodation

The special problems of delivering health care to an older population in a peripheral rural area are illustrated in the north-west Connemara project. People forego health care because of the need to travel long distances.

Forum's work points to the need for a system of health care specifically tailored to the circumstances of the remoter rural areas. Apart from more frequent clinics locally and better access to specialist services, this would include active participation by the local community - with some locals getting special training - in running resource centres (for the elderly) and day care services, supporting carers and improving access for isolated people.

In relation to housing for the elderly, there is need for a review of the arrangement whereby the local authority deals with a whole range of housing demands but the health boards are responsible for repairs to the homes of elderly persons. It is essential that people's requests in these matters are handled promptly by the appropriate agency.

PAUL identified a number of problems with public housing in Limerick, mainly arising from vandalism, lack of adequate maintenance and transient populations. It is pioneering a model of estate management based on the sharing of responsibility between tenants and the local authority.

Experience in both PAUL and Forum suggests the need for more professional, realistic and comprehensive assessments of housing needs than that which is carried out at present.

Among the groups most vulnerable to exclusion in PAUL's area are families under stress - lone parents, those with young children or with children in care. With the assistance of the Mid-Western Health Board, PAUL developed support networks for vulnerable families, including an innovative approach for parents with children in care.

Among Travellers, age-group mortality rates are higher than for the general population. This is due to inadequate health and accommodation - both of these factors themselves being closely related.

There is an urgent need for local authorities to take more seriously their responsibilities for providing accommodation for Travellers, and especially to speed up the provision of properly serviced halting sites.

Aspects of local development
All three projects devoted considerable resources to training, especially to building the capacity of their target groups to function effectively in collective action for meeting the groups' own needs.

Combating exclusion will require adequate resources for training in local community development and animation skills. An innovation by Forum was a one-year course in community development, accredited by University College, Galway. PAUL has also promoted greater access for tutors and learners to accredited opportunities.

In areas like north-west Connemara geographical remoteness, isolated communities and low population density make for difficulties in undertaking local development. Spatial exclusion is compounded by inadequacies in transport and communications.

There are several interests - public and private - providing or regulating rural transport but with little coordination of services and insufficient tailoring of provision to locally-specific circumstances.

Forum has prepared and recommended a pilot scheme to experiment with alternative models of rural transport provision, based on a closer integration locally of various services. The Irish Government's 1994 Budget allocated some funding for this.

PAUL's experience shows how urban housing estates, with poor infrastructures and amenities, result in high turnover of residents and consequent lack of a sense of community. These areas bear the brunt of economic decline and rising poverty. Urban renewal projects effectively by-pass them. The project has canvassed for a model of integrated urban development to address the particular problems of marginalised areas in cities.

An organisational framework for local intervention

In Poverty 3 the projects seek to avoid the dominant 'topdown', and sectoral approach in dealing with social exclusion. Instead, they emphasise local networking among statutory, community and voluntary interests, together with dialogue between the local and the national levels.

The Forum and PAUL projects are based on structured partnerships - organised in non-profit companies. DTEDG did not consider such a partnership form appropriate to its circumstances but, as an alternative, established strategic alliances with different allies depending on the actions to be taken. Structured partnerships presume a certain degree of local consensus about possible strategies and actions but DTEDG maintains that, as yet, the attitudinal basis for such a consensus does not exist in the case of work with Travellers. In DTEDG's experience there is need for the explicit recognition of Travellers in area-based developments. This must be supported by capacity-building among the local Traveller population and by the resourcing of area-based partnerships.

A locally-based partnership, coordinating the actions of several agencies, is more effective in combating exclusion than the autonomous actions of single-sector agencies taking decisions at a distance from the problems.

Experience in Forum and PAUL indicates that while partnerships of statutory agencies and voluntary organisations may easily be formed on paper, the successful operation of a *partnering process* requires training, commitment and good-will on the part of those involved. The voluntary sector, in particular, needs training and resources for its role in partnerships.

The commitment of concerned individuals to a partnership must be backed up by the institutional commitment of the individual's agency or organisation, ideally by a formal contractual relationship, specifying and confirming its obligations to the partnership.

Projects based on partnership need to give careful consideration to finding the correct balance between getting all the appropriate partners involved and avoiding fragmented and unwieldy structures.

Within partnerships, the projects show how the participation of target groups can be extended by a system of sub-committees and programme development groups.

Conclusion

The Poverty 3 Programme in Ireland will be the subject of an external evaluation later in 1994. The conclusions and recommendations emerging at this point are based very much on the projects' own internal assessment of their work. It is hoped that the issues raised here, and the more specific proposals made, will initiate a dialogue with policymakers and administrators and also inform the public debate on the processes of economic and social exclusion, and on the range of interrelated actions necessary to combat these.

The Editorial Committee
March 1994

AUTHOR'S PREFACE

This report draws out the lessons for policy and practice arising from the experience of the Third Poverty Programme (Poverty 3) of the European Union (EU) in Ireland (1989-94). There were three Irish projects in the programme - Forum model action project, North-West Connemara, Co Galway; PAUL Partnership, Limerick (People Action against Unemployment, Ltd) model action project, Limerick city (referred to as PAUL); and the Dublin Travellers Education and Development Group (DTEDG) innovative project. The model actions were large scale area-based projects, and the innovative projects in the programme had a focus on a particular theme or target group. Although the work of the projects as part of the Poverty 3 programme is due to conclude in July 1994, their activities are expected to continue.

The purpose of the report is:
1. to present an analytical account of the outcomes of the EU's Third Poverty Programme in Ireland, with reference to its relevance for policies dealing with problems of exclusion; and
2. to draw out the main lessons for policy and action at national and local levels under a number of key headings.

The report does not attempt to either describe the activities of the projects in detail or to evaluate their performance, but highlights the main lessons for policy arising from the programme.

The report was commissioned by the three Irish Poverty 3 projects, in conjunction with the Irish Research and Development Unit (RDU) of the Poverty 3 programme and the Combat Poverty Agency, the Irish co-funder of the programme. The researcher worked to an editorial committee consisting of Michael Mernagh (RDU), Patrick Commins (RDU), Mary Ruddy (Forum), Margaret Barry (Combat Poverty Agency), Jim Walsh (PAUL) and John O'Connell (DTEDG).

The many forms, dimensions and implications of social exclusion are the common threads of this report. The report begins with an introduction to social exclusion in Ireland (chapter 1) and to the Poverty 3 programme (chapter 2). It then discusses policy issues arising from the Irish projects' response to key forms of social exclusion in the areas of employment, education, civil and legal rights, health and accommodation, and local development (chapters 4-10). Chapter 12 highlights the organisational model of the projects. Chapter 13 summarises wider issues for policy and action at local, national and European level.

Local development initiatives, targeted at disadvantaged areas, are now a favoured element in national economic strategy, as evidenced by its inclusion as a separate chapter heading in the *National Development Plan, 1994-99*. This report provides a picture of one particular local model of development work and its aspects and potential in the specific context of combating exclusion and disadvantage. There are, in addition, important policy dimensions to local projects which are not often well understood or appreciated at regional and national levels. This account demonstrates the links between local actions and national policies and the implications for national policy formation.

The report is based on interviews held with key members of the projects and other experts, and on the written documentation of the projects, the Research and Development Unit, and the Combat Poverty Agency[1]. The report is a strategic document which brings forward recommendations for policy-makers and advisors, Government departments, members of the Oireachtas, the social partners and the community and voluntary sectors.

Brian Harvey
March 1994

---

[1] Those who kindly assisted in the research through interview or the provision of information were the following: Margaret Barry* (Combat Poverty Agency); Hugh Frazer (Combat Poverty Agency); Michael Mernagh* (RDU); Patrick Commins* (RDU); Kieran McKeown (consultant); Pauline Conroy Jackson (Central Unit); Jim Walsh* (PAUL); Sean McNamara (PAUL); Margaret Slattery (PAUL); Denis O'Brien (PAUL); Maggie Phayer (PAUL); John O'Connell* (DTEDG); Seamus O'Grady (Forum); Chris Curtin (Forum); Tom Lavin (Forum); Mary Ruddy* (Forum); Ena Coleman (Forum); Johnny Coyne (Forum); Janet O'Toole (Forum); Catherine Forde (Forum); Yvonne Keane (Forum) and Seamus Ó Cinnéide (European Observatory on Social Exclusion)
* Member of Editorial Committee

CHAPTER 1

Unemployment, poverty and social exclusion in Ireland

1.1   Introduction

Ireland is one of the poorest regions of the European Union; its GDP per capita being about two-thirds of the Union average. Those out of work total over 290,000 people, or 18% of the labour force, which is almost twice the European Union average rate. As in other European countries, the rate is unevenly distributed. In some working-class estates in Dublin, Cork, Limerick and Galway, unemployment rates of up to 80% are by no means unusual. In rural areas, problems of unemployment are compounded by underemployment and emigration.

1.2   Unemployment, poverty and social exclusion

The prime source of information on poverty in Ireland is the wide-ranging study carried out by the Economic and Social Research Institute in 1987 (*Poverty and the Social Welfare system in Ireland*, Dublin, Combat Poverty Agency, 1988). The purpose of the research was to lay down valid guidelines for the measurement of poverty in Ireland; to estimate numbers in poverty; and to classify those most in poverty or at risk of being so. The ESRI found that, taking a poverty line of 50% of average disposable income, equivalent to an income of £40 a week, 23% of the national population fell below that line. Comparable figures for other European countries suggest similar levels of poverty in Portugal and Greece, marking these three countries as a group with exceptionally high levels of poverty in Europe.

The ESRI classified those living in poverty and at risk of being so. A number of broad categories emerged. The main groups living in poverty were the unemployed (32.7% of the poor); farmers (23.2%) and the low paid (13.2%). The ESRI report confirmed an emergency link between poverty and unemployment and especially with long-term unemployment (by 1991, 60% of the unemployed had been out of work for more than one year).

Subsequent studies suggested two further important dimensions to poverty in Ireland. First, there was evidence that poverty affected women disproportionately (Daly, 1989). Furthermore, lone parents (principally women) were at a considerably higher risk of poverty. Second, households with children were at much greater risk than households without children (23% compared to 13%). By 1987, evidence had emerged that child poverty had risen considerably over the previous 20 years (Nolan & Farrell, 1990).

Other research conducted in Ireland over the past 30 years has identified groups living in extreme poverty, providing depth not available from the ESRI study. One of the main groups was the Travellers. Some detail is given here on the Travellers, since they are the focus of the Poverty 3 innovative project in Ireland. There are about 3,500 Traveller families in Ireland, numbering about 20,000 people (0.5% of the national population). Travellers have their own language, intermarry between themselves and have their own social customs. Travellers attempt to make a living through seasonal work, tarmacadaming and trading in old cars, scrap metal and batteries.

The living conditions of most Travellers are seriously inadequate by modern standards. Less than half of all Travellers are in settled accommodation, 6% live in prefabricated buildings and 50% in roadside caravans. Only 53% of all Travellers have piped water; 49% have access to a toilet; 38% have bath facilities. Poor living conditions are reflected in low standards of health: the infant mortality rate of Travellers is three times higher than settled people; 5% of Travellers live to 50 years and only 1.7% of them survive to the age of 65. The enrolment rate of Travellers in primary school is 75%; only 10% continue school after the age of 12; the illiteracy rate of adult Travellers is about 90%. Travellers suffer considerable discrimination, exemplified by the practice where many shops and pubs refuse to serve them.

1.3   A definition of social exclusion

Since the ESRI study was carried out, the debate on poverty in Ireland has been gradually redefined in terms of 'social exclusion'. Social exclusion is a much more dynamic concept of the processes of social change than 'poverty'. Social exclusion draws attention to its underlying causes as much as its manifestations. Social exclusion refers to the structures and processes which exclude persons and groups from their full participation in society. It explains that poverty does not just happen: it flows directly from the economic policies and the choices which society makes about how resources are used and who has access to them. The forces of exclusion change as economies and societies change. Social exclusion may take a combination of forms - economic, social, cultural, legal - with multiple effects. The term exclusion has connotations of process, focusing on the forces by which particular categories of people are closed off from the rights, benefits and opportunities of modern society.

Social exclusion is not just about lack of money, but may be about isolation, lack of work, lack of educational opportunities, even discrimination. The

3

notion of social exclusion has a strong policy focus: it is often the result of the ineffectiveness of policies, of the perverse effects of policies and of the distorting outcome of social class decisions. Social integration or inclusion, by contrast, is about drawing people into society in a number of different, complementary ways - into the labour market, into social services, into more equal relationships with their fellow citizens, into networks of care, companionship and personal and moral support[2].

Ireland shares problems of social exclusion with its partners in the European Union. The Irish projects are based first, in an area of rural depopulation; second, in a disadvantaged urban area; and third, in a project working with a vulnerable minority. Thereby they bring together three of the great European themes of social exclusion. In 1988, in *The Future of Rural Society*, the European Commission identified rural decline as a grave problem on a European scale. By the same time, the problems of the cities and of the quality of the urban environment had become recognised as critical throughout the member States. In the early 1990s, the treatment of minorities, discrimination and xenophobia had likewise become a worrying concern of governments and policy-makers.

This report records some of the ways in which the Poverty 3 programme found how people are socially excluded - and maps out some of the means of social reintegration.

---

[2] For a more detailed discussion of some of the themes of social exclusion in Ireland, see Ó Cinnéide and Corrigan, 1992 and Commins, 1993.

4

CHAPTER 2

The Poverty 3 programme

2.1   An introduction to Poverty 3

The Poverty 3 programme was the third of three programmes developed by the European Communities to combat poverty. The first ran from 1975-80; the second from 1985-9; Poverty 3 from December 1989 to June 1994. Technically, the title of Poverty 3 was 'the medium-term community action programme concerning the economic and social integration of the economically and socially less privileged groups in society'. Its budget was 55m ECU or IR£44m.

Poverty 3 contains two types of project: model actions and innovative measures. Poverty 3 has 29 model actions and 12 innovatory initiatives, spread throughout the European Communities. The Irish projects reflected this division: two were model actions (Forum and PAUL); one was an innovative measure (DTEDG). Fifty-five per cent of the budget of the model actions was paid by the European Commission, 45% by a national co-funder, in Ireland's case the Combat Poverty Agency; with the innovative measure, the balance was 50/50. The budget for the Irish projects was 4.8m ECU over the five year period, or IR£3.84m.

The innovatory measure was funded at a level similar to that of the projects of the first and second poverty programmes. The model actions, however, received substantially higher funding, about five times greater. In addition to funding as part of this programme, the projects were later able to draw in additional funding over the five year period. The projects also received continuous advice, help and support from the Irish RDU, the Combat Poverty Agency and the programme coordination body appointed by the Commission (called the Central Unit, based in Lille, France). The RDU provided technical assistance and developed the European links of the programme; the Combat Poverty Agency advised the Irish Government on the lessons emerging from the programme.

2.2   Aims and principles of the Poverty 3 programme

The aims of the Poverty 3 programme, as expressed by the European Council decision establishing the programme in 1989, were to produce organisational models for action to combat poverty, involving partnership between interested bodies in the areas concerned; to ensure the coherence of Community policies affecting less privileged groups; to strengthen economic and social cohesion and to be a forum for exchanges, stimulation and optimization of effort.

Poverty 3 employed a number of key concepts in its work. The model actions were especially enjoined to act on them. These were organisational principles of partnership and participation; strategic planning, multidimensionality and the targeting of specific groups of persons; and self-evaluation.

Partnership alluded to the requirement that projects be implemented by means of a partnership representing public and private organisations, agreeing jointly to engage in a coherent and agreed strategy. In Ireland, model actions sought partners in the local authorities and among State agencies; these organisations were represented on the management committee of the projects. Partners were expected to report back to their parent bodies, thereby cementing their involvement and making it more than the contribution of an individual. In Ireland, partnership meant a structuring of relationships with statutory bodies that went far beyond anything that had taken place up to that point.

Participation referred to the expectation that the target population, people living in poverty, would have an involvement in the projects. Each project was expected to find and devise means whereby the target population could participate, in some way or at some level, in the preparation, management and day-to-day operation of the project.

Multidimensionality referred to the ways in which projects were expected to address the many forms in which people are excluded from society. Exclusionary processes operate simultaneously on several facets of people's lives. Projects were expected to respond to this in multidimensional but integrated action. Multidimensionality draws out the strands of poverty beyond the immediate ones of income and employment, and explores the wider links to health policy, transport, accommodation and education, and undertakes counter actions in an integrated, systematic manner. The Commission stressed that the projects must not simply be a collection of unconnected, heterogeneous projects but a coherent programme of assistance crossing the limited frontiers of traditional anti-poverty projects to the wider political and administrative arena. The projects were expected to shed light on these wider links and act accordingly.

Self-evaluation required projects to have systematic procedures for taking stock of their progress, so that they themselves could assess the manner in which they were reaching their objectives. Each project was expected to set aside 5% of its budget for self-evaluation.

Regarding **targeting**, the model actions of Poverty 3 covered much larger geographical areas than the two predecessor programmes. For this reason, they were required not to spread their efforts indiscriminately. Model actions were expected to operate in depth, targeting their resources on those most in need and those most excluded.

The projects were required to produce a strategic plan, regular progress reports on their work and plans of work for the year ahead. The Commission stressed that Poverty 3 was a programme of actions: it was not simply a fund to be drawn on. Projects were issued with guidelines. They were expected to operate within a common framework; a discipline of ideas and organisation. It was expected that as a result of the programme, both the governmental and non-governmental participants would learn about social exclusion and its many dimensions, find new or more effective ways of combating exclusion and gain fresh insights which would lift the struggle against social exclusion to a new plateau of knowledge and effectiveness. The Poverty 3 projects were expected to follow the principles and practices outlined above in a structured, purposeful manner across Europe.

2.3   The Irish Poverty 3 projects: locations and aims

Forum is located in the west of the country, the project covering Clifden Rural District which has a population of 8,535 (1991 census) and a land area of 78,737 ha. The region has suffered a 50% population loss since the foundation of the State. The project focused on the problems of rural underdevelopment.

The specific aims of Forum, as listed in its *Plan of Work 1992-94*, were to:
- establish the scope and effectiveness of voluntary and statutory cooperation in jointly tackling issues of rural poverty and development;
- jointly implement a range of measures to tackle poverty;
- increase the capacity of local communities to become more involved in their own local development;
- assist communities to develop leadership and management skills in order to challenge social and economic isolation;
- disseminate lessons learned to the local population, community groups, statutory bodies and policy-makers; and

- incorporate and implement relevant new actions and programmes based on the project's experience.

This would be done by working with the following groups: the elderly, women, the unemployed and underemployed, young people and community groups.

PAUL is located in the southwest of Ireland in Limerick, the Republic's third largest city (pop. 76,000). The project's target population was drawn from four local authority housing estates in the north-west and south-east of the city, whose population is circa 20,000 people (Southill, St Mary's, Our Lady of Lourdes and Moyross parishes). The PAUL project expanded substantially in 1991 when it became part of the Government's scheme of 12 Area-Based Responses (ABRs) to long-term unemployment as part of the national Programme for Economic and Social Progress (PESP). This extended the PAUL target group to all long-term unemployed people in the city and added a fifth target parish.

The principal aims of PAUL, as listed in its *Strategic Work Plan 1991-94*, were to: promote the social and economic integration of the least privileged groups through innovative organisational models which emphasise partnership, participation and an integrated approach to tackling issues...The partnership is primarily concerned to address the issue of long-term unemployment and its impact on the lives of individuals and families in Limerick.

The DTEDG is located in the national capital, Dublin. There are about 20,000 Travellers in Ireland, of whom a quarter may be found in the Dublin area. The project focused on the problem of cultural discrimination.

The principal aims of the DTEDG, as enunciated in its *Strategic Plan 1991-94*, were to:
- support the rights of Travellers to self-determination and equality;
- build recognition of Travellers' self-identity;
- develop anti-discrimination policies and practices; and
- achieve dialogue between the Travellers and the sedentary population.

This would be done by working in two distinct ways - directly with Travellers; and with settled people.

2.4 The activities of the Poverty 3 projects

The three Irish projects developed a wide range of activities. They were:

Principal project activities of the three Irish projects in the Poverty 3 programme

Forum, north-west Connemara

- Resource centres and active age clubs for the elderly
- Support for the provision of bus services
- Coordination and development of aquaculture
- The establishment and support of women's groups
- Remedial education services, resource library,toy library
- Summer recreation and playschemes
- Advice, support and assistance to local community development associations
- Provision of adult education and training opportunities
- Coordination and development of local small scale tourism ventures
- Information-giving through seminars, workshops and meetings

PAUL, Limerick City

- Community action centres in four communities
- Welfare rights information service; benefit take-up campaigns
- Advice to people in debt
- Early education intervention project
- Adult education courses
- Project for lone parents
- Career relaunch for long-term unemployed over 25s
- Urban afforestation training programme
- Community childcare facilities; childcare training
- Support for and development of local cooperative
- Pilot project for the co-management of housing estate
- Network to support families whose children were in care

DTEDG, Dublin

- Training programmes for Travellers and professionals working with Travellers
- Educational events, information days, seminars and workshops
- Development of national and regional fora for Travellers (e.g. youth forum, women's forum)
- Health awareness programme
- Scheme for the improvement of standards in Traveller accommodation
- Traveller heritage centre
- National religious pilgrimage for Travellers

2.5 How the projects operationalized the concepts of Poverty 3

2.5.1 Partnership

Poverty 3 projects were expected to demonstrate new and effective means of combating social exclusion. Policy change would arise from the practical experience of the projects, but they were not expected to be lobbying organisations in themselves.

The model action projects work in partnership with other public and private agencies concerned with social exclusion. The partners of the two model action projects are listed in this diagram.

Partner organisations of the two model action projects

Forum, north-west Connemara

- Western Health Board (Programme Manager, Community Care)
- City of Galway Vocational Education Committee (Chief Executive Officer)
- FÁS (Regional Manager)
- Galway County Council
- County Galway Vocational Education Committee
- Connemara West - a local development company
- Bord Iascaigh Mhara (from January 1993)
- Teagasc (from January 1993)
- Nine local community organisations - Ballinakill, Ballyconneely, Cashel, Cleggan, Clifden, Inishbofin, Leenane, Recess, Roundstone

PAUL, Limerick City

Original partners
- Southill Community Services Board
- Southill Cooperative Development Society Ltd.
- Moyross Partners
- St Mary's Parish Awareness and Development Group
- Our Lady of Lourdes Community Services Group
- Limerick Youth Services
- Limerick Centre for the Unemployed (Now part of ICTU delegation)
- Mid-Western Health Board
- FÁS, mid-west region
- Limerick Corporation
- Shannon Development
- City of Limerick Vocational Education Committee

Additional partners following expansion in 1991 as ABR
- Department of Social Welfare
- Irish Business and Employers' Confederation (IBEC)
- St Munchin's parish
- Irish Congress of Trade Unions (ICTU)

The composition of the partnership was expanded by both model actions, new partners being added during the lifetime of the projects. Thus in its original form, PAUL comprised 12 partner agencies, run by a management committee of 17 members. In November 1991, it expanded to 15 partner agencies, its management committee being enlarged to 24 members, including staff representation and a chairperson. This report focuses on the Poverty 3 element of the project.

PAUL expanded in four other respects during the period. In October 1992, it was selected by the Department of Social Welfare as one of five Indebtedness Scheme Pilot Projects to provide advice on debt and moneylending to low-income families, becoming manager of a multi-agency Debt Forum comprising twelve advice, creditor, enforcement and welfare agencies. In March 1993, the PAUL project secured funding from the EC's HORIZON programme with the stated objective of the integration of lone parents into the labour market. PAUL attracted funding from the EC global grant for local development and from the Irish Government's Community Employment Development Programme.

Forum was a partnership of a long-standing community-based organisation, Connemara West, which had pioneered local development work in the area, together with nine representative community bodies, the main local authorities and the most relevant State development agencies operating in the region.

DTEDG took a radically different approach to partnership. It pointed out that the project was itself a partnership between settled people and Travellers. It added:

DTEDG has worked in partnership with the State by making some statutory programmes accessible to Travellers. However, until the State is prepared to address the issues of racial prejudice particularly in its institutional forms, the conditions are not present for a deeper partnership. In the meantime, DTEDG is prepared to put energy into addressing this issue through seminars, conferences, papers, meetings and negotiations. The fact that some government ministers and individual politicians support the group's work creates the possibility for further progress in the future. DTEDG is firmly committed to developing alliances with other relevant sectors in order to achieve the programme objectives.

2.5.2 Participation and targeting

In order to target its work effectively, Forum carried out a baseline study of NW Connemara area (Byrne, 1991). The baseline study was built on data from the national censuses, interviews with 140 low-income households and information collected from local voluntary organisations and State authorities. As a result, Forum identified the following target groups, upon whom it decided to concentrate its efforts over the following four years: elderly people; the unemployed and underemployed; women; young people; and community organisations.

Forum operated through five working groups corresponding to the target groups: the elderly; women; the unemployed and underemployed; and youth and education. It was the function of the working groups to maximize participation in the area where Forum worked. Working groups included representatives of community and voluntary organisations, users of the project, relevant statutory organisations and staff. The working groups had responsibility for implementing the Forum programme, reviewing progress and making recommendations. Each working group elected a representative to the board of directors.

PAUL operates through four subcommittees: finance; research & evaluation; action centres; and adult guidance, all chaired by members of the board of management; and through six programme development workshops (PDWs): economic activities; education & training; information & welfare rights; environment and cultural activities; family support services; and initial contact with the unemployed. Community action centres operate in the four target areas of the project.

DTEDG operated through five subcommittees: the Poverty 3 support group; youth and community work; women's issues; traveller economy; and cultural heritage.

Dublin Travellers Education and Development Group - DTEDG

CHAPTER 4

Employment, economic development and social exclusion

Unemployment is recognised by the Government, political parties and the social partners as the most severe socio-economic problem facing the country. It is probably the single greatest contributor to social exclusion. Exclusion from the labour market leads not only to reduced income but to exclusion from community life, education and other opportunities for self-advancement.

4.1   North-west Connemara

4.1.1   Unemployment, underemployment and social exclusion

In NW Connemara, unemployment and underemployment are significant problems. The main occupation is farming, comprising 35% of all people in the labour force, more than twice the national average. Most farms are small, run by single people and generate incomes of less than £5,000 a year. Incomes on several farms may fall well below £2,500 a year. The average size of farm is 30ha, two out of three being less than 12ha. In some districts, farms are even smaller. Four out of five farmers receive unemployment assistance. Most of the land is characterised as unproductive. Connemara has the lowest level of mechanisation of agriculture in Galway - less than one tractor per 404ha.

In one household in three the main earner is unemployed; 61% have been out of work for more than one year, 45% for more than five years. Further evidence of low incomes in the area is that 70% of the population has an income so low as to qualify for the general medical services ('the medical card'), compared to the national level of 37%.

The baseline report commented on the income problem in farming:

> Farmers engage in a number of strategies to survive. Having to negotiate the hurdle of conflicting state policies is an additional burden to the farmer. Farmers who increase herd numbers or sell stock run the risk of reduced or loss of social welfare and medical entitlements. The consequences for small farmers are the pursuit of farm activities which will entitle them to State subsidies but which ensures a life of poverty for this generation. Most farmers survive by combining farming with seasonal off-farm work, State transfers and welfare payments, together with contributions from other family members who may be earning off-farm incomes (Byrne,1991, p 106).

Most women in NW Connemara are involved in rearing children, farming, caring for elderly dependents, or domestic work. Some obtain limited opportunities in the services sector and tourism-based activities. Women have few opportunities to generate additional income or engage in small business activities. Both model actions recognize that the prospects of attracting industry into their localities are nil. Accordingly, they concentrated on maximizing the human and financial resources already in the area. Forum took two initiatives to develop the resources of the area - one in aquaculture, the other in tourism.

4.1.2   Development of resources

Forum supported the development of a number of shellfish-farming aquaculture projects. This work was done with Bord Iascaigh Mhara (BIM), the sea fisheries board, which from 1991 supplied a development officer and grant-aid. Forum set up three cooperatives with a membership of 130 people to produce oysters and mussels. A number of oyster beds have been established.

In doing so, Forum was conscious that the demand for Irish shellfish is increasing and the product is becoming better known in European markets. The bulk of fishery investment in the area to date had been in finfish farming, but this was under non-local ownership. The potential of shellfish farming had long been discussed, though little action had been taken. Shellfish farming is regarded as highly suitable in the local environment and economy: it is a clean industry, shellfish being reared in the wild. Shellfish farming can be accommodated within the demands of farming and seasonal tourism, making it ideal for coastal regions.

The Shellfish Development Officer worked from Forum's offices, attended coop meetings and monthly meetings of the Shellfish Development Committee, which comprised the cooperatives, BIM and Forum. Forum provided managerial, administrative, technical, planning and training support to the cooperatives. BIM and the cooperatives were very positive in their views on the benefits of having locally-based technical personnel working closely with shellfish farmers. BIM subsequently extended this model to four other coastal regions in partnership with LEADER and INTERREG projects.

But, Forum encountered a number of financial blocks to the development of successful small-scale oyster farming. First, the Department of the Marine imposes a licence fee. Generally, such a fee is in the order of £5,000 for a ten-year licence, or £500 a year. Second, considerable initial capital is required to maintain oyster beds before production. The amount required is at least £8,000. A 50% grant is available through BIM's pilot aquaculture grant, which means that £4,000 must be raised independently. Oyster beds take four years to produce marketable oysters (mussels take two years). An outlay of this size is prohibitive for the groups with which Forum works. In conjunction with one of the coops, Killary Mussel Coop, a novel method of overcoming this is being piloted. The coop has developed a leasing arrangement whereby rafts are leased to individuals, now coop members, who make repayments at harvest periods.

Relatively large financial outlay up front is an obstacle to the development of shellfish farming in such areas. Sympathetic leasing and payment systems, in conjunction with locally-based personnel provide a model of operation relevant not only to the fish farming economy, but to all economic developments which can contribute to sustainable employment and increasing revenue for low-income households.

4.1.3   Tourism

Tourism poses many problems as a means of raising incomes. First, due to the short season, it is likely to be a supplementary, rather than a main source of income or employment. Second, employment in hotels, shops and bars is generally unsatisfactory due to seasonality and low wages. Third, households on low incomes lack the relatively high investment they need to make their houses available for renting or taking in guests.

Forum made an original contribution to the debate on how Ireland's national tourism policy should be developed. The project commissioned a report on tourism in NW Connemara (Tubridy, 1993) which was a large-scale exercise in research, analysis and policy-making. There was wide consultation in its preparation (five well-attended public meetings), as well as a visitor survey and an inventory of local participation in the tourist trade.

First, the report outlined the tourism picture in Connemara. Connemara receives an estimated 400,000 bednights from tourists each year, generating about £27m in income. Surveys of tourists showed that they most appreciated the scenery, quietness, tradition and intact nature of the area. They were critical of the state of the roads, public toilets, noise in certain places, lack of medium-priced food, and badly trained bar staff. Bed and breakfast (B&B) is the most popular form of accommodation used for families and people over the age of 25.

Employment, economic development and social exclusion

Connemara provides hotel, self-catering and bed and breakfast accommodation for tourists, just under half the B&B and self-catering accommodation being approved and registered by Bord Fáilte, the Irish Tourist Board. To qualify for registration under Bord Fáilte, B&B accommodation must have three bedrooms and a separate bathroom and sitting room for guests.

Tourism in the area is administered by the Western Regional Tourism Organisation, known as *Ireland West*. It comprises the local authority and commercial bodies providing tourism services. Tourism development is funded nationally and under the EU's Structural Funds Operational Programme for Tourism. Such funding tends to support large-scale, special interest projects. There were only four applications to the last round of the Structural Funds (1989-93) from NW Connemara, of which two received funding. There was a fee of £100 to make an application. Funding for equestrian centres was given only to developers with at least 20 horses. With such a set of priorities, Forum says, it is possible for tourism traffic to increase, but for the numbers of people benefiting locally to fall.

Connemara, according to Forum, is an area of considerable tourist potential, combining natural beauty, a unique landscape, extensively managed land, wildlife, fauna and flora, as well as being clean and unpolluted. It has a long archeological and industrial heritage, a strong folklore and folklife tradition, historical and vernacular architecture and a literary and artistic heritage.

Forum drew up a £1.7m plan for community-led sustainable tourism which it defined as:

> tourism based on the region's unique environment and heritage, which will enhance the environmental, social and economic conditions of the residents, particularly low-income groups. The community will be able to influence how tourism develops and interacts with other sectors. This plan is targeted at low-income groups which comprise the largest single sector of the population (Tubridy, 1993, vol III, p 1).

The plan proposes the development of locally-owned self-catering accommodation, small camping sites, the relaxation of rules concerning B&B accommodation and support for family hotels. The plan makes specific proposals for improvements in water supplies, roads, clearing rubbish, landscaping and pathways, signposting and sewage treatment, to be coordinated by a tourism cooperative for the region. Sewerage and cleanliness are important issues: raw sewage is discharged directly into a number of bays in the area, and sewerage-need assessments are based on winter populations rather than summer ones. The Department of Social Welfare would be required to amend its rules governing unemployment assistance, to enable people to build up tourism-derived incomes. The plan proposes training in heritage-based tourism for local people. Finally, the plan would involve a development of local food resources and specialities. It would bring local people into the tourism planning picture and ensure that the lower end of the market was linked to the upper end.

The plan stated how important it is to be selective in the form of tourism that should be permitted:

> What is required is not major tourism infrastructure like interpretive centres, casinos or yachting marinas, but the maintenance of an authentic culture...
>
> The last operational programme for tourism [under the Structural Funds] would have offered little aid for the initiatives proposed under this plan. The level of support offered to individuals and community groups was not attractive (ibid, p 37).

The *National Development Plan 1994-99*, refers to the importance of environmental quality in tourism provision and culture and heritage measures. However, the emphasis of the £583m tourism plan is on the increase of revenue and tourism numbers, rather than the nature of the tourist product itself. The National Plan makes no reference to tourism being community-led or designed to assist people on lower incomes. The principal departure in the new Programme is the investment of £50m in a new flagship project, a national 2,000-delegate conference centre in Dublin.

Present policy in hotel development is to provide grant-aid for large hotels only. Under the first round of the Structural Funds, hotels must have 35 beds or more to be eligible for grant-aid. Over 1989-93, forty projects benefited from hotel investment of £61m, of which £6.6m came from the Structural Funds. When challenged on this policy in the Dáil, the Minister for Tourism and Trade replied that all the available money for hotel improvement would be spent overnight if small hotels were eligible. More jobs are created in large operations than small ones. According to the Minister, studies carried out by economists point out that the way to create more jobs in tourism is to attract high-spending tourists to large-scale facilities, though the Minister did not disclose the reports he was relying on.

There seem to be three problem areas here. First, Bord Fáilte does not see itself as having a developmental role. The main thrust of its work appears to be promotional. Second, existing tourism policy is focused on a very narrow product range, with investment concentrated at an inappropriate end of the market. Small tourism operators are specifically excluded from the investment programme. Third, the structure for the promotion of Irish tourism is exclusionary. Forum has the impression that the regional tourism bodies are heavily weighted in favour of large scale tourism projects.

Responding to the Forum plan, Bord Fáilte restated its policy that all accommodation should be licensed so as to meet the more demanding standards which visitors expect. It is aware that capital is hard to come by in disadvantaged areas and that this may cause difficulties. It had introduced a new 'specialist' category of approved one-bedroom accommodation on west coast islands.

The Forum plan has important implications at EU level. Under the first round of the Structural Funds, £2,000m was committed to supporting tourism development in Objective 1 regions. Several Community Initiative Programmes have provisions for tourism-linked projects: LIFE, LEADER, INTERREG and FORCE. Furthermore, the Commission launched a three-year £33.5m Community Action plan to assist tourism in January 1993. It is interesting to note that the plan refers to the importance of small tourist businesses and how tourism must respect the natural environment, cultural heritage and 'the integrity of the local population' (OJ L 231/16, 1992). It seems that the Irish Government's current approach is at odds with the decisions of the European Union.

Forum does not know if its report represents a unique approach - indeed it suspects that its approach is shared by other community projects in other parts of the country. Some members of both Bord Fáilte and the Department of Tourism and Trade have responded positively to it at a personal level.

4.2   Limerick City

4.2.1   Unemployment and social exclusion

Limerick city and its immediate environs account for 9,800 registered unemployed people, about three quarters of the unemployed in the county and two-thirds of those out of work in the mid-west. Of this total, 3,900 people are long-term unemployed (40%). Unemployment has trebled in Limerick since the start of the 1980s and is the outstanding issue facing the city. The unemployed are concentrated in local authority areas, where the average unemployment rate is twice that of the entire city (45% to 21% in 1986).

The labour market in Limerick has experienced major restructuring in recent years. Traditional industries in the city have closed, to be replaced by high tech enterprises. In addition, new industries have located in the county, well outside the city to the south west, and in the Co Clare industrial parks based around Shannon Airport to the north west. There continues to be a drift of people from the city area outwards to the suburbs - 7.5% between 1986 and 1991. Some of the new industries are high technology, for example, those located in the aerospace industry. Limerick has been characterised by significant internal job substitution, several city jobs now being done by contractors out of the city (e.g. construction, electrical work). Limerick thus has a number of dormant, obsolete and inappropriate skills.

4.2.2   Helping people out of unemployment

The PAUL Partnership has prioritised measures to tackle long-term unemployment in its strategic work programme. Five initiatives have been undertaken:

i.   Job creation projects (both self-enterprise and community business);
ii.   Job placement agency;
iii. Innovative training and educational programmes;
iv.   Outreach programmes; and an
v.   Adult guidance service.

In responding to unemployment, PAUL provided support for unemployed people to help them start their own businesses. This programme was introduced in October 1992 under the Government's Area Allowance Scheme (AAS). This permits unemployed people starting their own business to retain their social welfare allowance in their first year while generating income from a new business. It is a requirement of people starting their own business under the AAS that they register with the Revenue Commissioners and, if need be, for VAT. One of the effects of this has been to bring people out of the black economy and 'go legitimate'.

In addition to operating the AAS, PAUL provided a financial package to people starting their own businesses. This comprised:
- grants for feasibility studies, up to £5,000 or between 75% and 100% of the costs;
- equipment grants up to 100%, including second-hand equipment;
- employment grants up to £5,000 per job;
- technical assistance; and
- the guarantee of loans in credit unions.

This package was more generous than those on offer from the main State development agency in the region, Shannon Development: its range of support is generally 50% to 75% of costs and excludes second-hand equipment and the service sector.

PAUL believes its approach is flexible, client-based and responds to that area of the economy where jobs are growing fastest, namely the service sector. In the period November 1992 to November 1993, PAUL spent £236,000 supporting 81 enterprises (averaging about £2,900 each).

In parallel with this, PAUL, in cooperation with FÁS, operated a business appraisal course. The course was designed to equip people with the skills necessary to run their own business and back them up when they became established. Subjects covered included presentation, communication, administration, insurance, law, market research, financial planning, book-keeping, tax and computers. PAUL states that as a result of its work, it has assisted 110 unemployed people to set up their own businesses.

Three particular issues have arisen as a result of this work. First, the AAS combines a positive package to which unemployed or underemployed people are able to respond. Second, the range of mainstream State support services for people to start their own business are not comprehensive, flexible or generous enough to suit people at the lower end of the labour market. The positive response to the PAUL package reinforces this impression. Third, there is considerable growth potential for services jobs in this part of the labour market. Hitherto, support for indigenous job creation has concentrated on manufacturing because of its high added value compared to other employment. The wisdom of such an approach must now be open to question in the light of PAUL's experience. These are important considerations for the Government task force on the service sector and for the European Commission, whose policies have stressed the potential for Small and Medium-size Enterprises (SMEs) and the service sector in economic development.

The project has also highlighted a number of policy issues, primarily through its research programme. The main theme here was a review of the effectiveness of Government provisions for the long-term unemployed.

4.2.3 Effectiveness of Government provision for long-term unemployed

The Government's principal labour market measure to combat long-term unemployment during the period of Poverty 3 was the Social Employment Scheme (SES). The Scheme provided temporary part-time employment to unemployed persons aged over 25 years who had been out of work for more than twelve months. The income received was broadly similar to the level of unemployment assistance. The PAUL project questioned the value of the SES scheme as a means of combating social exclusion.

SES is funded by the State training agency, FÁS, but operates in each area through local sponsors, which include public bodies and a wide range of non-profit community-based groups and organisations. PAUL reviewed the operation of the SES in Limerick in a substantial research study (Ronayne & Devereux, 1992). The main findings of PAUL's research were:

About 300 people were employed on projects in Limerick city, or about 10% of the long-term unemployed in the city.
* Sponsors found the SES imposed additional financial burdens;
* no training was provided on a number of schemes; few workers were able to use their existing skills while participating in the SES;
* over a quarter, 29%, regarded their working conditions as 'very poor'. These numbers came disproportionately from those participating in schemes operated by the local authority;
* although SES workers received more income while on the scheme than while on unemployment assistance, some SES workers lost the secondary benefits they would have kept had they stayed on unemployment assistance;

- although SES workers could obtain part-time income for the hours when they were not participating on SES, in practice very few were able to;
- few SES workers (23%) received career advice or support while on the scheme;
- there was little evidence that SES was meeting its central aim of helping people find work. Less than 20% found long-term work after they left SES. For older and educationally disadvantaged participants, the scheme seems to have had no positive benefit, either from the point of view of improved skills or of obtaining employment.

The study concluded that the SES, as operated, was 'not contributing to an improvement in the employment prospects of many participants'. This was attributed to a downswing in the labour market, low vacancy rates, recruitment patterns and the fact that what jobs were available required skills far beyond those available to most of the long-term unemployed.

In 1992, SES was replaced by the CEDP (Community Employment Development Programme) in Limerick city as part of the ABR initiative. PAUL believes that CEDP incorporates many of its recommendations for reform, such as:

- the improved quality of training in CEDP (now totalling twenty days a year, with an allowance of £100 to attend approved training outside the project);
- the retention of secondary benefits, including Christmas bonus, medical card, differential rent, fuel and butter vouchers;
- careers advice from the course supervisor; and
- changes in eligibility to allow lone parents and young unemployed to participate on CEDP.

4.3   Travellers
4.3.1   Economy and social exclusion
Most Travellers are dependent on social welfare; only a small number are employed in waged activity. Travellers prefer self-employment and income generating activities which revolve around street markets, trading in old cars, collecting and selling batteries, tyres and other forms of scrap. The DTEDG took a specific initiative resourced through the PESP Area-Based Response, to respond to the marginalization of the Traveller community in the economy. It sought to combine Travellers' existing but not well understood economic activity in the field of scrap work with new economic and environmental trends to recycle goods and products.

Since the mid-1980s, there has been increasing public demand in Ireland for the recycling of such products as paper, glass, household waste and batteries. Recycling of newspaper, glass and plastics is still relatively new in Ireland. The present paper waste recovery rate is only 18%, with glass at 27%.

In Ireland, the Department of the Environment has, since 1989, encouraged recycling schemes through 50% start-up grants for the recycling of glass, paper, cans and plastics. Since 1989, the DTEDG-based Travellers Resource Warehouse (TRW) at Pavee Point, Dublin, has benefited from this scheme. TRW recycles paper, cardboard, wool, lace, timber and plastic, all of which are collected from businesses around Dublin. The TRW recycles these materials to provide creative arts materials for schools and community groups in the Dublin area. The DTEDG believes that its work is important in the shaping of attitudes toward Travellers, for there is thought to be a widespread public belief that 'Travellers don't work'. It is interesting that within the Traveller economy, recycling has been a viable self-sustaining economic activity for years, whereas there is a general acceptance that start-up costs for recycling in the settled economy require underwriting grant-aid from Government.

Recycling had always played an important role in the economy of the Traveller community, although Travellers themselves have not generally used the word 'recycling'. The main items in which Travellers trade are ferrous metals (steel, cast iron, car bodies); non-ferrous metal (aluminum, lead, zinc, copper, tin and brass); fabrics (clothes), car parts, lawnmowers, and household items (furniture, refrigerators, washing machines, pots and pans). The Traveller economy is based on self-employment, on mobility of labour and transport and of the integration of home space and work space. Items are collected door to door, from dumps, or from engineering sources and small factories. They are sorted, stored and recycled to merchants and traders in the settled community. Dealing with ferrous metal alone, up to 50% of scrap metal which goes to the Irish steel industry is derived from Travellers: it totals 75,000 tonnes and is worth about £1.5m, generating ultimately about 400 jobs in the settled economy.

The Traveller economy has traditionally appeared to outside observers as chaotic and disorganized. This is not so. It is a structured, flexible economy. Part of this appearance is due to fluctuations in market prices: Travellers store goods when prices are low, selling when they are higher. This has implications for social welfare schemes, which assume a consistent level of means (or the lack of them).

DTEDG recommends a number of changes in Government policy which will ensure an expanded role for Travellers in recycling (see Tennyson, 1993):

- access by Travellers to landfill sites to obtain scrap;
- financial packages which reflect operating rather than start-up costs;
- an end to discrimination against Travellers by insurance companies;
- facilities for recycling, sorting and storage at halting sites (at present some local authorities prohibit this); and
- legalization and regularization of Traveller recycling within the social welfare and employment code.

These are important details. The DTEDG has recorded instances of the authorities requiring Travellers moving into housing in Cork to sign a contract agreeing not to collect scrap. In 1992, it was reported that halting site families in Killarney would be strictly screened and if Travellers wanted to bring in scrap, 'that was too bad, the rules would be strictly enforced'. Dublin County Council had an agreement with a private contractor to remove scrap cars from Traveller sites.

DTEDG insists that the Department of the Environment, in drawing up its recycling strategy, recognize and draw on the existing record, tradition and expertise of Travellers. It would be ironic if, in the course of making the recycling sector formal and structured, policies were to be adopted which squeezed Travellers out of an area of economic activity which they have pioneered. DTEDG has warned that this is a real danger. Likewise, the European Union, in its future environmental and waste management policies, must recognize the value of the Traveller economy in this area and support Traveller recycling pilot projects. In its submission to the European Commission on the future social policy of the European Union, DTEDG asked the Commission to provide support for the social economy sector at a time of economic restructuring, and to acknowledge the distinctive forms of work engaged in by Travellers and Gypsies.

Meanwhile, a national recycling strategy document is expected in 1994, followed by a Waste Management Bill. DTEDG has asked that the Traveller economy be made an integral part of such a strategy.

4.4   Policy issues

First, the model action projects restated the links between unemployment and social exclusion. Although the response of the model actions to unemployment had a number of features in common, there was an important distinction between them. Although PAUL and Forum both spoke of unemployment, Forum specifically used the term 'underemployment'. It did so largely on the basis of the baseline study which argued that the strategies of income maintenance adopted by people in Connemara were complex and crossed traditional distinctions of unemployed/employed. Forum's model formed a basis for its economic regeneration work in aquaculture and tourism. There have been positive outcomes to PAUL's efforts to tackle unemployment. The Area Allowance Scheme is the beginning of a process which adjusts the social welfare and tax system to encourage a return to the workforce without penalty.

The projects' work with unemployed and underemployed people demonstrates the potential of viable economic development by people living in conditions of extreme poverty. PAUL outlined how services-based self-employment is possible in economically disadvantaged urban areas. In a similar manner, Forum demonstrated the potential of the aquaculture industry in an economically disadvantaged rural and maritime area. DTEDG demonstrates the potential of recycling as an income-generating economic activity by Travellers. Most such economic activity will probably be achieved through self employment or SMEs. SMEs have been promoted by the Commission as an essential element in future European economic growth strategies.

All three projects draw attention to the blocks preventing progress in generating economic activity. In Limerick, these include the range and nature of State supports and the lack of readiness to support the service sector. In Connemara, they concern licensing and access to capital. In the Traveller economy, the challenge is for the State to acknowledge and resource the Traveller economy with its emphasis on self-employment and income generation as opposed to waged labour. The area of recycling is an obvious example but DTEDG is exploring other possibilities, including finding ways to increase Traveller participation in waged activities. One of the most promising areas which could be developed is the local services sector where work of a socially useful nature could be undertaken if properly subsidised. State policies must adapt in the light of these findings.

Employment, economic development and social exclusion

PAUL drew specific attention to the defects of the Social Employment Scheme. In addition to a number of complications in its interaction with the social welfare system, it is largely ineffective in its objective of reintegrating workers into the labour market, entirely so for men aged over 45 years. Other aspects such as training and entitlement to benefits such as medical cards seem to have been addressed by the CEDP which has replaced it in the 12 ABR zones in the country. Despite the evidence of its shortcomings, SES remained an important element in the Government's response to unemployment.

In the 1994 budget, the Government announced the replacement of the SES and the CEDP with a new programme called Community Employment. The degree to which Community Employment will remedy the defects of the SES and build on the improvements of the CEDP remains to be seen.

Forum's tourism study was recognised by the Minister for Tourism and Trade as - in his words - a radical, thought-provoking contribution to the development of tourism policy. It is more than that. It begins to answer troublesome questions that have been raised as to why, in the face of considerable tourism investment and the presence in Ireland of growing numbers of tourists, low-scale providers in remote areas have not benefited as well as was expected. Forum suggests some answers: the existing structures of grant-aid, promotion, regulation and control have operated in such a way as to exclude people on low-incomes. More seriously, EU tourism funds seem to have been cornered by the very top end of the tourism market. The pursuit by Government of a big-is-beautiful, environmentally-stressful policy contradicts the advice presented by ecologists, economists, scientists and social analysts for the last twenty years.

Forum makes a case for an integrated, environmentally sensitive, democratically accountable, socially equitable, economically profitable approach tied to market needs and research. It is a model which has a ready applicability in other European peripheral economies. It is frustrating that there is as yet no evidence of changes in policy at governmental level.

CHAPTER 5

Social welfare and social exclusion

Social welfare provision is a vital part of the day-to-day lives of those targeted by the three Irish Poverty 3 projects specifically by those affected by social exclusion generally. Socially inclusive services make people feel part of society and full citizens. Services which are poorly administered, which discriminate, which fail to respond to real needs, add to a sense of exclusion from society. From 1986, when the Government-appointed Commission on Social Welfare made its report, there has been a lively discussion in Ireland on how social welfare services can be made more adequate to meet real needs, more simple to understand and operate and more efficient.

5.1 Limerick City

5.1.1 Exclusion in the Social Welfare System

An important function of the model action projects was to inform people of their welfare rights. These projects are an important source of information to supplement and complement the existing work of the Department of Social Welfare, health boards and Citizens' Information Centres run by the National Social Service Board (NSSB). The PAUL project serves principally the local authority housing estates of Limerick Corporation: of the 3,200 Corporation tenants, 84% are dependent on social welfare for their income, half of whom draw unemployment benefit or assistance. About 16% of Corporation tenants are employed, about 33% of whom are classified as low paid.

Information on social welfare rights and entitlements was an important aspect of PAUL's work. Between 1990 and 1992, the community action centres dealt with 1,217 queries about welfare rights and entitlements. Despite the many simplifications of the social welfare system which have taken place over the past 10 years, the projects continued to draw attention to anomalies and deficiencies within the system. Two were highlighted by PAUL.

First, PAUL argued for a contributory welfare payment for widowers. Under the social welfare code, a widow receives a contributory pension based on her own and her late husband's PRSI contributions, and is entitled to earn from work in addition. No similar scheme was open to widowers. However, a contributory pension has now been introduced for widowers in the Government's 1994 Budget.

Second, PAUL was active in supporting appeals. Representatives of the project accompanied claimants to appeal hearings, giving the claimant confidence and providing important background and local information for the hearing. Of the 12 appeals taken by PAUL in 1992/3, all were successful. A PAUL-represented claimant won compensation at an Employment Appeal Tribunal unfair dismissal hearing.

This activity stresses the continued value of community-based projects in providing social welfare advice and support to people in disadvantaged communities and in exposing deficiencies and anomalies in the system. The value of welfare advice services has already been noted elsewhere, as has been the importance of assisting people with appeals. This work is labour-intensive and is often underfunded and undervalued.

5.1.2   Privacy and procedures

PAUL drew attention to the lack of privacy for interviewing in health centres and in the offices of the Department of Social Welfare. The Department of Social Welfare in fact had interviewing rooms available but these were not advertised to claimants. PAUL requested the Department to inform all local claimants that they could request interviews in consulting rooms; this was agreed.

PAUL asked for improvements in the treatment of recently-bereaved social welfare claimants. This followed reports by claimants that when reorganizing their claims in the week following their partner's death they had been treated unsympathetically (although not incorrectly). A new procedure was introduced whereby following the death of a claimant, the welfare officer would call to the partner's home to set the claimant's affairs in order, thus reducing the person's distress. A feature of both these issues was that both the Department of Social Welfare and the Health Board seemed entirely unaware that their existing procedures were causing frustration or difficulty. These actions by PAUL strengthen the case for funding community organisations working on social welfare issues.

5.1.3   Debt

Debt is a priority area of work for PAUL. Moneylending was a serious problem in the local authority housing estates in the city as low-income families were unable to access more conventional credit sources (e.g. banks). Pressure on the Health Board and the Society of St. Vincent de Paul charity suggested that debt was pervasive among low-income families. Furthermore, of the five local authority housing estates served by the project, only one has a bank. Most tenants are not in a position to offer security for loans.

In 1992, PAUL was approved by the Department of Social Welfare as one of five Indebtedness Scheme Pilot Projects. The project established a multi-agency debt forum comprising 12 advice, creditor, enforcement and welfare agencies. The project had four specific elements:

- provision of a money advice service;
- liaison with creditors on repayment and default procedures;
- the development of new sources of credit; and
- promotion of the rights and responsibilities of credit consumers.

The project helped families to manage their debts but did not pay people's bills for them. The service was free and confidential; it offered a scheme whereby people could pay their debt in a planned way through special accounts with the local credit union. People were encouraged to save a small amount each month with the credit union so that they might borrow from this source rather than go back to money-lenders.

In 1993, the project published the *Money Advice Handbook*. PAUL also recommended a toughening of legislation to control moneylending in the long-delayed Consumer Credit Bill (it was eventually published in 1994).

5.2   Travellers
5.2.1   Social welfare and exclusion
The Travellers project found itself confronting one of the most socially excluding aspects of the Social Welfare Code. Since the mid-1980s, all Travellers not living in conventional houses have been required to sign on for social welfare at the same time throughout the country (11.30 am on Thursday mornings). 'Signing on' is the process whereby people claim and collect their unemployment entitlements.

When the new local employment exchanges were being established in suburban areas of Dublin, it was intended that Travellers would continue to draw the dole at the city centre offices. As a result of lobbying work, Travellers are now able to access their Social Welfare payment in many of the local employment exchanges. However, there are some problems emerging where payments are made through post offices, which once again highlights the need for an anti-discrimination practice in institutions and agencies for minority ethnic groups like Travellers. In Dublin, Travellers other than those in standard housing who apply for Supplementary Welfare Allowance are obliged to travel to Castle Street in the city centre. This necessitates considerable travel from outlying county areas. Thus 'settled Travellers' may attend locally whereas the majority, 'non-settled' Travellers, must go to the EHB clinic in Castle Street for their allowance.

This system is explained on two grounds. First, it is rationalized on the basis that the Castle Street service can provide a service dedicated to Travellers and specially orientated to their needs. Second, when the service was set up, the then Minister for Social Welfare justified it on the basis of a 1981 Department of Social Welfare report which found that Traveller abuse of social welfare was a significant and growing problem. Special control measures were required. Travellers were never consulted about the report; its existence was not known until 1985, by which time the new measures were well in place. It has never been published.

The Travelling community is the only group in the country subject to these special control measures. Research by the DTEDG found that the system is detested by the Travellers who are required to use it. DTEDG and other Traveller support groups tried to negotiate with the Government on this but without success. DTEDG ran a number of campaigns against the Castle Street system, but dropped them for fear of retaliation against individual claimants participating in protests.

5.3   Policy issues

The money advice and welfare rights work of PAUL underscores the importance of local information, advice and advocacy services in the overall context of Irish social welfare provision. It provides real and valuable day-to-day help and support to people on low incomes. The Government should reinforce the role of advice services such as those provided by the projects, the Free Legal Advice Centres, CICs and similar bodies.

PAUL has been to the vanguard in encouraging the State to fund appropriate responses to problems of debt, which have been a widely-known problem associated with poverty in Irish society for many years. PAUL's pioneering indebtedness project represents a concrete, clearly thought out response to the problem. It combines immediate assistance and a preventative framework with alternative credit sources. How effective it will turn out to be remains to be seen. The debt project raises much larger questions concerning the level of legal protection for consumers against illegal or unethical money-lending and the appropriate legislative framework for responding to money-lending.

The discriminatory delivery of social welfare services for Travellers is a form of administrative social exclusion.

CHAPTER 6

Education and social exclusion

Education is central to the issue of social exclusion. If organized according to principles of justice, solidarity and equity, the education system can ensure access to education by all social groups, minorities, geographical areas, all ages and both genders. Education can provide new opportunities for training, reintegration to the workforce and training for citizenship and community participation. Conversely, education can exclude because of financial barriers, ineffective location of services, or disproportionate investment in some types of services. Patterns of allocation of educational resources can perpetuate or worsen exclusion; or they can provide routes which integrate students of all ages into society. Education was a central theme of the Poverty 3 programme in Ireland.

6.1 North-west Connemara

6.1.1 Exclusion in North-west Connemara

The baseline study identified early school leaving as a significant problem in Connemara. Few parents send their children to pre-school - many do not believe it is necessary and for the rest it is not possible due to cost and transport problems. About a third of school-going children have problems in reading and writing. Parents are unhappy about the absence of remedial facilities and regard this as the greatest single gap in provision. A third of parents expressed dissatisfaction with their children's school for physical reasons: dampness and cold, lack of indoor toilets and lack of playing facilities are the most frequently cited reasons. There are few parent-teacher meetings. Many parents express great scepticism about the ability of the education system to equip people for the realities of the present labour market.

6.1.2 Education for children and young people

The project decided to give priority to the needs of pre-school children, children with remedial needs; and young people and adults.

There are seven pre-schools in Connemara, all of which charge a fee to cover costs. Forum supported playgroups which catered for between six and twenty six children each (68 in all). All playgroups were hampered by limited funding. Fees for the playgroups are part-paid for unemployed parents by the Western Health Board. The Department of Education does not appear to recognize that it has a responsibility here.

Forum believed that a priority area of its work should be remedial education. It is estimated that one child in three has difficulty with reading, writing or other aspects of learning. At that time, there was only one remedial teacher for the 14 national schools within its area of work catering for 973 primary school students. Remedial needs ranged from the slight to the severe and included some children with mental disabilities. Forum joined in the efforts of schools and parents to get additional remedial teachers allocated to the area. This did happen in 1992 and there are now three resource teachers which means that all schools now have a remedial service at least once a week. Forum has continued to have an involvement in meeting remedial education needs through its teachers resource centre and library in Clifden. Remedial materials are very expensive: current Department of Education policy is that there is a grant allocation of £125 per resource teacher, not per school, for the purchase of remedial material. Forum invested £4,000 in materials which were not otherwise available to teachers and resource teachers. The library contains graded reading materials and workpacks for reading and mathematics, as well as a toy lending library used by the playgroups.

In additional to the remedial work, Forum was intensively involved with classroom teachers in running a series of training workshops which were designed in close cooperation with teachers themselves. The training workshops were recognised by the Department of Education as official inservice training. The resource centre was also used by teachers for photocopying and basic presentation of material to which most schools would not otherwise have access. To ensure the continuation of the service, Forum applied to the Department of Education to have the resource centre recognised as a full educational resource centre with a full-time coordinator.

Forum ran a youth programme in cooperation with the Foróige youth work organisation. Forum's work highlighted the lack of a statutory youth service, or anything to match that of Comhairle Le Leas Oige in Dublin. The Vocational Educational Committee provided a £1,000 once-off payment toward youth activities, but the real cost, Forum estimated, was about £6,000. Forum provided a range of sports activities in nine centres for over two hundred youngsters in the 5-14 age group. Funding was requested from the youth and sports section of the Department of Education, but this was not forthcoming.

6.1.3   Adult education
Forum provided a range of adult education classes - by the end of 1993 it had provided 27 classes in six centres for about 330 - 340 people,

representing about 7% - 8% of the adult population. These classes covered such diverse areas as art, computers, childcare, dance, Irish, tax, photography and metal work. Successful participants in the advanced computer classes were awarded City and Guilds Certificates. In addition, women participated in three FÁS-funded enterprise courses, places being oversubscribed by a 2:1 ratio.

Forum wished to involve the widest possible range of participants in the programme. A profile of those who attended Forum's adult education courses was carried out (O'Toole, 1993):

- two-thirds were women (69%);
- the largest single age group was the 30-39 age cohort;
- 12% had left school at primary level, 4% at intermediate level, 43% at secondary level; and
- two-thirds were employed, one third unemployed.

Before the start of the project, the level of provision of adult education was very low in the area. The Vocational Education Committee, responsible for adult education, had only one organiser in west Galway for adult education, literacy and youth programmes. Forum believed that helping parents with literacy difficulties to read and write also proved to be of enormous benefit to their children's academic performance.

6.2 Limerick City
6.2.1 Educational exclusion in Limerick
Early school leaving is a dominant feature of the poorer parts of Limerick city. In the public housing estates, 38% of the adult population left school at 15 years of age, compared to 18% in the city as a whole. There is evidence of close links between early school leaving and unemployment: in one parish, Moyross, of 179 young people aged 19 to 21 years registered as unemployed with FÁS, only 15% had a Leaving Certificate.

PAUL views preventative and corrective measures as vital if these young people are not ultimately to become the long-term unemployed in the first decade of the new century.

6.2.2 School costs
Theoretically free, in practice parents meet a range of school related costs. These are 'voluntary' contributions toward building and maintenance and

the charges for text books, extracurricular activities and clothing and footwear associated with the start of the school year. PAUL carried out a study of the costs of primary schooling (O'Donoghue, 1991). The purpose of PAUL's study was to focus on the educational costs faced by low-income families, seeking to quantify their extent, to detail how families coped and to ascertain their use of various welfare schemes which assist with such costs, and to see if there were any specific policy interventions which could help.

There are a number of existing schemes to meet education costs for low-income families. These are:
- the Clothing and Footwear Scheme;
- the School Books Scheme;
- the School Meals Scheme; and
- Exceptional Needs Payments for First Communion and Confirmation.

The Clothing and Footwear Scheme and the Exceptional Needs Payments are administered by Community Welfare Officers (CWOs) employed by the health boards (in Limerick, the Mid-Western Health Board) and delivered in health centres. Exceptional Needs Payments are made at the CWO's discretion. The Clothing and Footwear Scheme operates under defined national criteria and a means test, the allowance then being £25 for a child in primary school and £40 for a child in secondary school. The School Books Scheme is run at the discretion of school principals. The Department of Education allocates block grants of up to £9 per child to schools where there are 'necessitous' pupils. The School Meals Scheme is organized by the local authority, half the cost being recovered from the Department of Social Welfare.

PAUL's research was based on information provided by 99 families with school-going children attending schools within the target area. The principal finding of the research was that the average annual cost per child for uniform, footwear and books ranged from £63.36 (4-6 year olds) to £123.66 (13+ years). There were additional annual costs for school outings and activities ranging from £23.60 to £65.72 and for lunch and transport (between £374 and £912.60). First Communion and Confirmation costs were in the order of £105.40 and £144.36 respectively. The consequence, as described by PAUL, was that households are unable to meet the costs from their weekly income and up to a third are forced into debt. Other effects of these costs are family disputes, strains on mental health and cutting back on other household necessities, including food.

Knowledge of the four schemes varied considerably. Only one of these schemes, Clothing and Footwear, was actively promoted by the Department of Social Welfare. There was evidence that people did not apply for schemes because, although they knew of them, they either did not have enough information to apply or presumed that they were ineligible. For those who did receive assistance towards costs, PAUL's research found that the level of assistance fell far short of the actual costs involved. Fearing stigmatization, between 8% and 14% of respondents did not apply for schemes even though they knew of their entitlements and were in need. PAUL's research found that of those families who did not think themselves eligible for Clothing and Footwear, half went into debt to meet these costs; for those who did not think themselves eligible for Exceptional Needs Payments, a third borrowed.

There was dissatisfaction with the delivery of schemes in health centres. Claimants reported having to wait over two hours for interview; that the conditions were cramped and lacked privacy; and that up to three visits were required to make a claim. The report states:

> What is common to all four Schemes is the discretionary nature of entitlement - though applied to varying degrees. This aspect attracted a very negative response, with two-third of families feeling they had no rights, were required to beg or feel ashamed. The majority of respondents visualized an application for discretionary help as some form of personal plea for help and comparable to asking for charity or a handout (O'Donoghue, 1991, p 15).

A further dimension to the problem concerns low-paid families. Those at work are generally not eligible with the exception of the Clothing and Footwear scheme, which was extended in 1991 to include working families receiving Family Income Supplement (FIS) or on FÁS schemes.

PAUL's study concluded that education costs are a major burden for low-income families, whether at work or dependant on social welfare. The existing schemes designed to meet these costs fail in their take-up rates and their adequacy. These shortcomings are even more serious, for they persist even after Child Income Support is taken into account.

PAUL proposed seven reforms to meet the educational cost burden for low-income families:

- existing schemes to be publicised, with benefit take-up campaigns;
- application forms to be more widely available and processed in one place;
- Clothing and Footwear, Exceptional Needs Payments, Meals and Books to be available as of right to all Medical Card holders;
- payments to cover the basic costs of supporting children at school (PAUL suggests a clothing, footwear and uniform allowance of between £40 and £60; a combined school books and school activities payment of £30 to £50; and a First Communion payment of £80 to £100;
- improvements in the School Meals scheme (e.g. hot lunches);
- child benefit payments to be doubled in September, December and March to help families with school-related costs; and
- efforts to minimize educational costs for families with school-going children, such as school rental schemes, fewer changes in school books, standard uniforms and allowing children to make their First Communion and Confirmation in school uniforms.

PAUL estimated that should these proposals be met nationwide, the costs of the Clothing and Footwear, School Books and School Meals schemes will rise from £9.7m a year to £36.2m a year (separate costings of the First Communion/Confirmation Exceptional Needs Payments are not available). Double child benefit in the three months proposed would add a further £34.9m.

The report led to three results. First, payments under the Clothing and Footwear Schemes were increased by £10 per child to £35 (primary) and £50 (secondary). Second, there was a streamlining of the process whereby claimants for back-to-school clothing and footwear allowances had to make up to three visits to the Health Centre. As a result of PAUL's representations, the health board operated a new system in Limerick which required only one visit. It also advertised the Scheme. This led to an 18% increase in take-up of the back-to-school clothing and footwear allowances in one year.

Third, the Department of Education decided to grant eligibility for the School Books Scheme to any recipient of the Clothing and Footwear Scheme. The new arrangement was scheduled for introduction at the start of the school year in September 1992. The introduction was postponed until September 1993 and subsequently deferred a second time until September 1994. It is speculated that school principals have obstructed the change, wishing to retain control of the administration of the schools-based scheme at a local level.

PAUL's research is important in adding to our knowledge of education costs. It describes the exclusionary manner in which some services are administered: some social welfare services are delivered in ways that people find stigmatizing, time-wasting and humiliating. Administrative complexity is evident in the way in which four procedures are used for four schemes in which the applicants and levels of entitlement were quite similar. PAUL argued that the use of one existing means test, that of the Medical Card, would eliminate the need for all the others and has the advantage of using a simple, well-understood system that would maximize take-up and permit low-paid families to benefit.

6.2.3   Prevention of early school leaving, and accreditation of adult learning

PAUL has devoted considerable attention to the problem of early school leaving, mainly through two initiatives. The first is an early education intervention project attached to a local primary school. This project seeks to bring about sustainable improvements in the educational attainment of 78 target children by devising, implementing and evaluating a curriculum with a pronounced academic emphasis tailored to meet specific needs. The initiative is unique in contemporary Irish education. It addresses many of the current concerns of teachers, parents and educationalists, which are also central to the debate on education which has been ongoing in this country since the Green Paper on Education was launched.

The second is a strategy to develop accreditation procedures for adult learning, including those who currently tutor in this field of education. The project has established links with local, national and international organisations with an interest in the assessment and accreditation of adult learning. From this networking, new models are being piloted which indicate a significant new policy development in second chance education.

6.3   Travellers
6.3.1   Exclusion from education

Traditionally, Travellers educated children at home in their own community. It was a break in their tradition to send Traveller children away to school. Traveller children's experience of school is mixed: some schools welcomed them; some ostracised them; others refused to enrol them. The results of

Traveller participation in the education system have generally been disappointing. Whereas some teachers have adapted to the needs of Traveller culture, many more have not. Traveller attendance at school can be erratic.

The DTEDG favours Travellers being educated alongside their settled peers. They stress the importance that teachers have intercultural teaching materials available to them and the skills to use them appropriately and effectively.

At present, 4,000 Traveller children out of an estimated 5,000 are enrolled in primary schools. Of those enrolled, just over half attend special, segregated classes while the remainder are in ordinary integrated classes. DTEDG is critical of the segregated classes, especially when these have children of mixed ages and abilities and are not linked to the mainstream system. The information on enrolment does not show the low level of attendance of many Traveller children and the tendency for schooling to be disrupted for any number of reasons - nomadism, evictions, child labour, social events within the extended family, parents' illiteracy, Traveller alienation from the school system etc. The result is that, according to teachers' opinions (Blackrock Teachers Centre, 1993) many Traveller children leave school at a level which is three years behind the norm in core subjects[3]. Poor attendance is partly responsible for this but the failure also lies with the school ethos, the curriculum, the teachers, the teaching methods used and the poor living circumstances of many Travellers.

There are an estimated 2,000 Traveller children in the 12 - 15 age group. Of these only 90 are in schools and about 200 others enrolled in eleven special Junior Training Centres (Blackrock Teachers Centre, 1993). Of this small group which go on to second level schools, the vast majority leave after one or two years.

6.3.2   Exclusion from education decision-making
A central part of the work of the DTEDG was devoted to ensuring that Travellers and their spokespersons were represented on bodies which take decisions concerning them in the educational field. By doing so, it hoped to ensure that the Irish education system would be intercultural and, for Travellers, appropriate.

---

[3] Report of the EC Intercultural Education Project (Blackrock Teachers Centre, 1993).

In *Education and Travellers*, the Irish Travellers Movement (supported by DTEDG) proposed that:

Agencies such as the Department of Education, religious bodies, diocesan and other management authorities, teachers unions, youth organisations and parents organisations find ways to include Travellers at all levels of planning and administration, from local to national (e.g. National Council for Curriculum and Assessment), to boards of management.

DTEDG, with the support of the Department of Education, has also been involved in the provision of in-service courses for teachers throughout the country and resources schools and pupils who request information about Travellers.

The DTEDG pressed for, and was given, representation on the Task Force on the Travelling Community set up by the Minister for Equality and Law Reform (1993). Its members attended the Task Force's Subcommittee on Education. In Autumn 1993, it persuaded the Task Force to adopt recommendations on the education of Travellers. DTEDG contributed to the draft text of its first report and recommendations and the report was subsequently adopted (January 1994).

The National Education Convention, held on 11-20 October 1993, was organized by the Minister for Education. It was the first such national education conference of its kind and a special initiative of the new Minister. When the convention was first announced, DTEDG asked to be permitted to make a presentation to the convention as part of a tripartite group representing DTEDG, the Irish Travellers Movement and the Association of Teachers of Travelling People (ATTP). However, the Minister declined, stating that only the 'major' education partners would be designated as participating organisations.

It is difficult to understand why the DTEDG was not given the direct opportunity to make a presentation on educational areas directly within its remit as part of the Poverty 3 programme, nor why the ATTP's expertise was not felt to be of merit. At the same time, other organisations, whose brief is primarily dedicated to non-educational questions, like the Irish Creamery Milk Suppliers Association, were given greater prominence, status and influence at the convention. It appears that not only was an opportunity to make Traveller education a more important aspect of Government education policy missed, but that the Travellers and their teachers were treated in a socially exclusionary manner. In the event, a Traveller managed to make a brief presentation to the final hearing of the convention, through a backdoor route. This was done by DTEDG member Martin Collins when a place was given to him in the name of the Education and Training subcommittee of the Travellers Task Force through the cooperation of the National Parents Council. He spoke to a mini-hearing of 25 delegates (cf. Report).

DTEDG believes it is in a strong position to propose education reforms in Ireland on the basis of international agreements to which the Irish Government is a signatory and on the basis of Irish documents and agreements. The principal ones are as follows:

- the United Nations Convention on the Rights of the Child, 1989, which affirmed the right of the child to his or her own cultural identity, language and values and to enjoy his or her culture and language;
- the EC resolution of the Council and Ministers for Education for school provision for Gypsy and Traveller children, 1989;
- recommendations 21 and 23 of the European Parliament Committee of Inquiry into Racism, 1990, recommending educational programmes to promote an appreciation of minority cultures and develop teaching materials which provide instruction on racism;
- article 42 of the Irish Constitution, requiring all children to receive a minimum moral, intellectual and social education and requiring the State to provide free primary education;
- rule 10 of the Rules for Irish National Schools which specify that 'no child may be refused admission to a national school on account of the social position of its parents nor may any pupil be kept apart from the other pupils on the ground of social distinction'; and
- the Council of Europe Plan of Action to combat racism, xenophobia, anti-semitism, intolerance, and religious discrimination (October 1993).

DTEDG contributed to four international EU conferences concerning the implementation of the 1989 EC resolution in the member States. Their conclusions (made in Navan, Co Meath in 1993) were that:

There were little or no effort made by the various member State governments to publicise the resolution and felt this reflected a general attitude of disinterest in the issues concerned and the non-recognition in general of Travellers and Gypsies as minority groups.

However, first signs of change were evident in September 1993 when the Irish Government, reporting to the European Commission on the implementation of the resolution, admitted that 'much remains to be done' to improve Traveller education. It also undertook to host a major European Conference on Intercultural Education in May, 1994.

6.3   Policy issues

The work of the projects highlights the bizarre manner in which other branches of Government compensate for educational under investment by the Department of Education. Just as PAUL in Limerick shows the manner in which the Department of Social Welfare and the local authority pay school-going costs for low-income families, so Forum shows how the Western Health Board pays for preschool costs. Such a pattern invariably distorts national education strategies.

The experience of the projects shows how entire areas of education, like playgroups, pre-schools, adult education, literacy and youth work are largely dependant on voluntary pressure to get services going. The Department of Education does not see itself as having a pro-active or primer role in these fields which are so important from the point of social exclusion. In the £1.6bn 1992 national education budget, 36.7% is spent on primary education, 38.3% on second level, 22% on third level and 1.5% on 'other programmes'. The experience of Poverty 3 is that the 'other programmes' area is grossly underfunded and under supported. Such underfunding is a counterpoint to the hunger for adult education which the projects have unearthed.

In responding to early school leaving and the lack of confidence in the national and secondary school system, Forum invested in developing those areas of education where it can exert most influence: pre-school education, remedial education, youth work and adult education. Whether this will create a climate in which formal schooling eventually becomes more relevant, more effective, more attractive and more attuned to peoples' needs in the long term remains to be seen. And although adult education and second-chance education may have limited applicability in the labour market, their potential as a strategy against exclusion though community-building should not be underestimated. The work of the PAUL Project has identified new approaches to the problem of early school leaving - both preventative measures within the formal school system and remedial actions through adult education.

PAUL's research casts light on a hitherto little-studied aspect of social exclusion: school costs. The study provided, probably for the first time, a systematic assessment of these costs for low-income families in the Irish urban environment. It reveals serious flaws in the complex system of social welfare schemes which are designed to assist low income families in meeting these 'hidden' costs. PAUL suggested that these costs introduce exclusionary aspects to education which, ultimately, contribute to negative attitudes toward the education system and, indirectly, to early school leaving. This research is one of the significant discoveries of the programme. It poses a challenge to the Irish State to make education genuinely free at point of use. Forum also raised questions of financing and investment. In an area of sparse and declining population, like north west Connemara, the national policy on education fails to take account of the specific conditions such as the needs for grants for remedial teachers, and local resource centres with photocopying facilities.

DTEDG has highlighted the urgency of the educational needs of Travellers, particularly Traveller children of pre-school and primary school ages. A comprehensive approach is required in order to enable Travellers to participate in, and benefit from, the education system: properly resourced and standardised pre-schools; an adequate Traveller teacher support service; the production of curriculum and resource materials which respect cultural diversity; pre-service and in-service teacher training.

The Traveller project breaks new ground in educational policy for two reasons. First, it raises serious questions about the structure of decision-making in Irish education policy. The extraordinary resistance it encountered in trying to make a modest contribution to what was billed as a wide-ranging national consultation on education demonstrates a distinct lack of openness in these structures and highlights these structures as an exclusionary process in themselves.

Second, DTEDG used international instruments, which respect and resource cultural diversity, as a basis for seeking improvements in the education system in Ireland. The use of these instruments is by no means unusual in Irish advocacy work, especially in the human and social rights field, but the DTEDG may presage a new departure in educational politics. In the course of doing so, it made links with the Traveller and Gypsy groups throughout Europe whose cultural identity is often undermined or denigrated in schooling systems. From them, it becomes apparent that Gypsy education has many problems in common throughout the Union.

The work of the projects confirms depressing international commentaries on Irish education performance. 1993 OECD figures show that in comparison to our European neighbours, Irish people are relatively under-educated, leave school earlier and attend college proportionately less. Participation of mature and part-time students is low. The Poverty 3 programme has confirmed the centrality of education in combating social exclusion, inequality and disadvantage in Ireland.

Forum

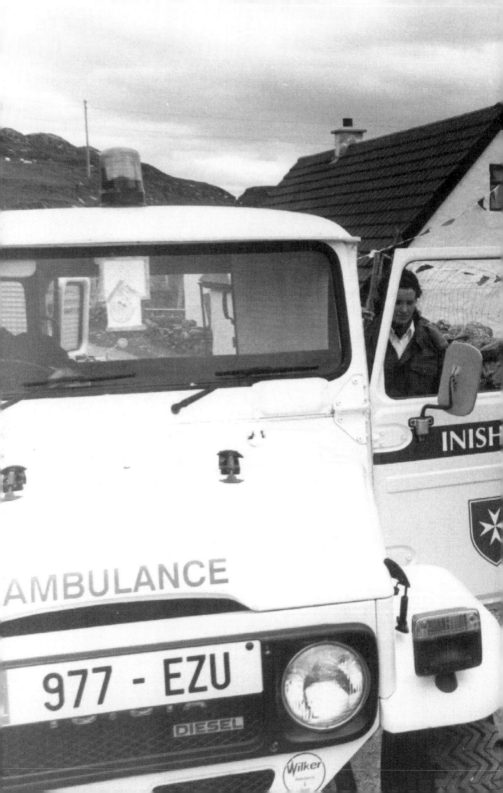

Legal and civic rights and social exclusion

Exclusion takes many forms. The most obvious forms are economic and social: these traditionally receive the most attention. Much less notice has been given in Ireland to the manner in which political, civic and legal mechanisms exclude people from society. The work of the DTEDG made significant progress to bridge that gap for Travellers. The Forum project demonstrated how geographic isolation was compounded by exclusion from the airwaves.

8.1   Travellers
8.1.1   The model of exclusion
The work of the DTEDG concentrated on persuading the Irish Government and settled people to change the manner in which Travellers are perceived. Until recently, Travellers had been perceived entirely as a 'problem' group with a chaotic, antagonistic and disruptive lifestyle. DTEDG affirms Travellers as a distinct group with valid, different and positive values which other Irish people should appreciate and which Irish law and administrative practice should honour and respect. This is a significant paradigmatic shift, one which, if brought to conclusion, is likely to have lasting value in a society which is perhaps the most homogeneous in Europe.

8.1.2   Changing the model
The full burden of this undertaking is apparent if we consider that Government policy, as expressed in the Commission on Itinerancy (1963) was:

> to consider what steps should be taken to provide opportunities for a better way of life for itinerants, to promote their absorption into the general community and pending such absorption to reduce to a minimum the disadvantages to themselves and to the community resulting from their itinerant habits.

Travellers were perceived as social drop-outs, misfits or deviants for whom absorption into the settled community was the solution. In the 1980s the language and nature of work with Travellers shifted. A fresh Government approach was spurred by the increasingly frequent clashes between Travellers and the settled community over sites. The Government's Travelling People Review Body (1984) used the term 'Traveller' rather than the term 'itinerant' which many Travellers resented. It adopted a working definition of Travellers as a distinct group 'with their own distinctive lifestyle, traditionally of a nomadic nature, but not now habitual wanderers. They have needs, wants and values which are different in some ways from those of the settled community.'

The Report recognised the desire of some Travellers to remain in halting sites, but warned that if they did, they could not expect to avail satisfactorily of health and welfare services. The review body declared emphatically that it was *not* seeking the enactment of anti-discrimination legislation.

In the years following its foundation in the mid-1980s and before the Poverty 3 programme, the DTEDG moved to a redefinition and understanding of the Travellers' position. This came from a prolonged period of reflection and theoretical analysis. Its axiom was that travelling, or nomadism as it was, and is, frequently referred to in Europe, is a valid way of life in itself, one that could and should be accommodated and respected in Irish society. Travellers have distinctive values, customs and language, an extended family tradition, and a distinctive work ethic which combines living and workspace. Travellers are a culturally distinct group and their different approach is not some form of poverty-related subculture which would disappear if their hardships were to be alleviated. DTEDG categorised as racist the practice of treating Travellers as inferior and not respecting their distinctive values; it labelled as similationist and ethnocentric the processes of forced settlement or the educational absorption of Travellers.

DTEDG believes that policies of integration, absorption and assimilation have failed. Many Travellers moving into settled accommodation in the 1960s on foot of the *Commission on Itinerancy*, earnestly hoped that integration would work for them. All the information reaching DTEDG was that it did not: 'settled Travellers' reported that they still felt they were an underclass in their 'new' communities. They were never accepted, and in 1993, 'settled Travellers' still reported incidents of being barred from pubs and commercial services.

The introduction of the concept of racism into the Irish public discourse has been a specific aim of DTEDG. Because Irish society does not see itself as having ethnic minorities, it therefore cannot see itself as acting in a discriminatory manner, since there is nobody to discriminate against. Until the late 1980s, any debate on discrimination in Ireland focused entirely on religious minorities. In broadening the debate, DTEDG developed a firm academic base for its challenge, circulating many papers, reports and discussion documents to underpin its model (perhaps the most succinct example is *Ethnicity and Irish Travellers*, by John O'Connell, DTEDG, October 1991).

8.1.3   Changing presentation

This shift in perceptions and approach has not been purely an ideological, theoretical, political or academic debate.   It has taken place through media work, dialogue with the authorities, policy proposals, posters and publications. A small sample includes, for example:

> *Traveller ways, Traveller words*, a book in which Travellers themselves described their past, present and future;
>
> *Pavee Pipers and Players*, an exhibition on the Traveller contribution to Irish music;
>
> *Pavee Pictures*, a photographic record of Traveller life and culture; and
>
> *Nomadism Now and Then*, which records Travellers' views on their lives.

Visual images play an important part in this process. Photography was used by the projects not, predictably, to reinforce images of helplessness amidst squalor, misery and oppression (that would have been all too easy) but to convey the portrait of individuals and communities surviving, living and working.

The redefinition of the Traveller in Irish society was accompanied by a series of measures to affirm Travellers' culture and heritage.   These included the establishment of the Traveller Heritage Centre in Pavee Point, Dublin; the Traveller National Arts Festival, held in May 1993 under the aegis of the EU's *Kaleidoscope* programme; slide shows on Traveller women, nomadism, flower-making and tinsmithing; four, week-long, national Traveller religious pilgrimages to holy shrines; and obtaining airtime from the national radio station, RTE, for a weekly programme on Traveller issues, presented by Travellers.

Considerable change is evident in the language with which political leaders in Ireland now speak of Travellers. Not only is the term 'itinerant' no longer used in public administration, but political leaders such as former Taoiseach, Charles Haughey, and the current Social Welfare Minister and Finance Minister have all spoken publicly about the need to respect and affirm the identity and traditions of Travellers.   An example of the change of official attitudes was evident when the Minister for the Environment opened the first exhibition of the Traveller halting site design awards. His comments mark the closest point to which settled Irish society has come to making amends for its treatment of the Travellers:

Overcoming prejudice and building a positive image is necessary but it's not easy. In the past we've shown ourselves to be adept at categorizing and pigeon-holing vulnerable minorities. Categorizing made life easier but didn't bring much joy to the people who inhabited the category. We must plan with travelling people rather than for travelling people. We must develop an understanding of their diversity and of their distinctive culture. To build a fully integrated, inclusive society we must at last try to come to terms with this nagging stubborn issue which has been with us so long.

8.1.4   Changing the law

For DTEDG, making a reality of Traveller identity and culture requires legal reinforcement. Legal provisions are wanted for two reasons: first, to bring to an end discrimination against Travellers in employment and in daily life; and second, to set standards for public administration and attitudes. Law is not just a reflection of attitudes, but it can inspire a further change in attitude in itself.

Travellers have long complained of personal discrimination in shops, supermarkets, pubs, hotels, petrol stations and other places which refuse to serve them and are abusive to them. Accordingly, DTEDG campaigned for Ireland to ratify the UN Convention on the Elimination of all Forms of Racial Discrimination. Ireland is the only member of the European Union not to have ratified this convention. The *Programme for Government*, adopted by the Government elected by the Dáil in 1993, gave a commitment to the ratification of the Convention. The Programme gave a pledge to pass equal status legislation to prohibit discrimination. In November 1993, the Minister for Equality and Law Reform told the Dáil that two Bills would be introduced in 1994. One would cover employment discrimination, the other non-employment areas such as goods, facilities, recreation, entertainment, transport, professional services, accommodation and property. Discrimination by a publican against a Traveller would be prohibited.

Prohibitions against discrimination are, said DTEDG, a matter of justice, affecting day-to-day living and commerce. Many Travellers experience great difficulty in obtaining insurance for their vans so that they may lawfully trade. DTEDG found that some insurance companies specifically name Travellers as an 'unacceptable risk'. DTEDG itself experienced difficulty in getting insurance for the van for the Traveller resource warehouse ('As soon as the word Traveller entered the conversation, brokers and insurance companies came up with a range of excuses for refusing to quote. A quote was eventually obtained from a broker who was unaware what the 'T' of TRW stood for').

The 1989 Prohibition of Incitement to Hatred Act made it an offence to incite hatred against Travellers. This was the first acknowledgement that legal protection for Travellers was necessary. In 1993, pressured by the DTEDG, the category of 'membership of the travelling community' was added to grounds for unlawful dismissal under the Unfair Dismissals (Amendment) Act by the Junior Minister at the Department of Enterprise and Employment.

The DTEDG, together with the Irish Travellers Movement and the Irish Council for Civil Liberties drew up the Draft Equality (Protection against Racism) Bill, 1993, as a model which might form the basis of the Government's own legislative approach.

8.2   North-west Connemara
8.2.1   Exclusion from the airwaves
An important element in the original Forum project was that it would have access to a local community radio service, to be known as North Connemara Community Radio (NCCR). The radio would operate under the aegis of the Connemara West company, Forum supplying a worker, programmes and finance for training needs. The failure, after five years, to obtain a licence to run a community radio service, is one of the greatest disappointments of the project.

From 1985-9, Connemara West, then sponsor of a project in the Second European Programme against poverty, intended to use radio as a means of opening up the debate about the future of NW Connemara and of providing information about community activities in the area. NCCR had built up experience of operating a radio station, being on the air for three months in the period before regulation (1988). At the start of Poverty 3, it had a studio and transmitter in place, strong local support and experience of what was involved.

The proposed station would be on air three hours a day. There would be a high level of volunteer contribution. There was a commitment to high quality content, local information exchange and Irish music. Other aims were to provide community groups with a medium for the regular and reliable flow of information; to provide a high standard education service; and to combat isolation and loneliness, especially for the elderly and housebound. The radio would be used as part of the Forum adult education programme.

NCCR stressed that its project was not just a proposal for a local station carrying local news, but for a broader vision of democratic public broadcasting. It would be owned by the local community and would promote access to the local community.

Broadcasting in Ireland is regulated under the Broadcasting Act, 1960, which licences State radio and television; and the Broadcasting Act, 1988, which regulates independent broadcasting. The 1988 Act established the Independent Radio and Television Commission (IRTC) which was then expected to licence a national independent television station, a national radio station, county radio stations and community radio stations. In a relatively short period, the IRTC issued licences for the first three categories (including 25 county-based radio stations) but awarded no licences for local community radio stations. Eventually in 1992, the IRTC licensed two experimental local stations, both in Dublin. The main one, Anna Livia Radio, was given a one-year licence (county stations have a seven-year licence) and was prohibited from earning advertizing revenue. NCCR made a fresh application in April 1993, with the backing of the partners on the board, the Department of Social Welfare, the Combat Poverty Agency and commercial interests in the area.

The IRTC never explained its failure to allocate licences to local radio stations. It is suspected that the Commission came under pressure from the commercial county radio stations not to allocate additional licences, for fear that this would undermine their lower than expected advertizing base. Another possible explanation is that the board of the IRTC comprised people who were unsympathetic to community development. The IRTC had 10 members, all of whom were urban-based, eight coming from Dublin. There were no rural members or representatives of the community sector. Either way, the project was deprived of its media arm. The refusal of the IRTC breaks a commitment by the then Minister for Energy and Communications, that 'the number of stations will be constrained only by the willingness of people to invest in local and community radio stations and the availability of frequency assignments' (letter to NCCR, 22 September, 1987).

The failure of NCCR to obtain a licence was a setback for the project. Hopes that a licence would eventually be granted rose in February 1994, when the IRTC invited proposals for 18-month pilot community radio services. However, they will be too late for the Poverty 3 programme.

Forum disputes the notion that the existing network of county radios has saturated the airwaves. The presence of over 14 pirate stations known to be operating in mid-1993 is further evidence of the desire of people for local community-based radio. Ireland has a relatively low ratio of stations to people compared to other countries.

NCCR has asked that the new board of the IRTC reflect the community sector; that it licence a specifically identifiable community sector; that there be a levy on the commercial sector to finance the community sector; and that a general licensing consideration be the degree to which a new station adds to the diversity of programming already in existence.

The new IRTC board advertised in February 1994 for applications for community broadcasting. There may be some opening up of access for community groups in 1994.

8.3   Policy issues

DTEDG believes that the public discourse on Travellers changed fundamentally over the past 10 years. Even if many people still have difficulties with concepts of Traveller culture and even if the location of sites continues to be the occasion of bitter conflict and local clashes, few political leaders at national level are now prepared to argue policies of assimilation. The national debate on Travellers in Ireland has, at least in part, been redefined around a political, civic and legal framework.

The work of DTEDG raises three important questions concerning future anti-poverty programmes. First, it raises questions about the suitability of the language of 'integration' - the terms of Poverty 3 refer to the 'integration of least favoured groups'. For some groups living in extreme poverty in the EU, the term 'integration' has had a number of nasty historical overtones. It should be used carefully: for small minority groups, integration must be largely on their terms, for if not, it constitutes absorption.

Second, racism is not a specific term of reference for the Poverty 3 programme. The Irish experience shows how racism is at the root of the experience of Irish Travellers and is probably the single most important element in their social exclusion. DTEDG found, in the course of its transnational work, six other projects in which racism is an important concern. This must be recognised in future anti-poverty programmes. Now that the European Parliament has adopted a resolution on xenophobia and racism (popularly known as the Ford Report), there is a firm institutional base for the next programme to recognize racism as an important element in social exclusion.

Third, DTEDG demonstrates the value of funding for groups engaging in advocacy and media work. While the DTEDG provided services, training and other activities for and with Travellers, the main thrust of its work was advocacy, analysis, theory, and representation. Moreover, the achievements of the DTEDG have been constructed on a small budget. The recommendations of the Irish Government's Task Force on the Travelling Community (January 1994) adopted many of the approaches, views and conclusions of the DTEDG. They show how a local group can affect change at the highest level in a relatively short period.

Finally, the work of the DTEDG illustrates that there is a place in the anti-poverty programme for projects which have a legal dimension in the struggle against social exclusion. DTEDG devoted considerable effort to building up legal protection for excluded people. This is a relatively under-used strategy in Ireland, though not in other countries. The growing interest in the EU in adopting legal norms to underpin social protection suggests that this work merits further growth.

Access to the airwaves is not a conventional battleground for the debate on social exclusion. This may be the first time that the regulatory environment for radio has featured in such a discussion. The experience of the NW Connemara project makes a clear case for a change in the way in which the Independent Radio and Television Commission operates in Ireland and for community radio to be seen as part of the processes of social inclusion throughout the Union.

CHAPTER 9

Health, accommodation and social exclusion

Access to quality health care and accommodation makes a society inclusive. Exclusion takes place when health services are inappropriately or inequitably delivered or where financial or other barriers are placed in the way. People may be excluded from housing through neglect or lack of suitable financial or legal means to provide for or improve their accommodation.

9.1   North-west Connemara
9.1.1   Health and housing
Older people, as a general rule, put health services under greater pressure than younger populations. In NW Connemara, there is a substantially older population than the national norm, 17%.   One detail is that the proportion of elderly males living alone is three times the national average (in some parts, 40% of the entire population consists of single males).

Bad housing is a significant feature in NW Connemara. Achievements in Irish house construction over the past 30 years obscure the fact that a core of poor quality housing remains a problem in urban and rural Ireland.   In Connemara, 7% of households lack electricity, 12% lack water, 17% lack indoor toilets and 18% lack a bath or shower. In some areas, these figures are much higher. Residents express the desire to have their houses repaired and improved - but they lack the means.

9.1.2   Delivering health services
Information on the health of residents was obtained by the baseline study and also by a study of primary health care in Ballyconneely in 1993 as part of a primary health care project run in conjunction with the Department of Community Health, Trinity College Dublin, and sponsored by the Western Health Board and the Combat Poverty Agency. The baseline study indicated that the most frequent medical problems arising were:
- for women, periodic depression, isolation, loneliness and resignation;
- for mothers, problems associated with childbirth and miscarriage;
- for the elderly, asthma, bronchitis, high blood pressure and incontinence; and
- for children, accidents, allergies, speech difficulties, hearing and sight problems and breathing difficulties.

Forum studies of consumer responses to the health service indicate that consumers are very satisfied with the quality of care provided; rather, the problems are those of access and distance. Many elderly people live in isolated areas without access to transport. Many elderly people are unused to leaving their houses and taking part in community activities.

Forum set up resource centres for the elderly in Letterfrack, Roundstone and Leenane and worked with groups of elderly people in Cashel, Recess, Clifden, Cleggan and Inishbofin. The resource centres provided hot meals with occasional visits by the public health nurse (PHN), chiropodist and hairdresser, and regular social events and outings attracting about 130 regular users and up to 270 participants for some of the social events.

Problems of physical remoteness are compounded by the low rate of telephones in households. In Ballyconneely, 33% of all residents did not have a phone, nor did 25% of those living alone. Forum provided a telephone subsidy system, which up to 30 elderly people availed. The PHNs identified elderly people at risk without near neighbours. The project offered to pay about half of the £130 telephone installation fee.

The project provided two pilot meals-on-wheels schemes in Clifden, Inishbofin and Ballinakill. The Inishbofin and Clifden services were discontinued due to lack of demand. The Ballinakill scheme continues to operate successfully. It enables housebound older people to be identified and subsequently contacted by those attending the centre. Those to whom meals are delivered can see it as part of a larger programme and not a focused charity or highly stigmatized service.

Dental services are another health problem area. The Ballyconneely study found that 58% of people do not avail of a dental service. A public service is only effectively available for school children in the 5-12 year age group. There is a long waiting list for orthodontic treatment. The waiting list for dental services under the general medical services scheme is eight to nine months. There is no private dentist for 80km. Water in the area is not fluoridated, and although some areas had been prioritized for treatment, the area of the health study is not one of them.

Forum worked with Galway County Council and the Western Health Board in examining ways in which responses to the elderly's needs for housing repairs and upkeep may be made more effective. At present both bodies are involved in such repair work. The Western Health Board deals with special housing aid which is confined to repairs only and rarely exceeds £2,000. The

County Council deals with a range of housing demands, but Forum, because of its contact with the elderly and with public health nurses and home helps, has been in a position to integrate responses. With the help of the public health nurses a priority list of 23 houses in need of repair was submitted to both bodies; up to that point the nurses dealt only with the health board. The Council accepted the priority list, agreeing to operate the priorities outlined.

The baseline study identified how one of the greatest regional problems was the need to travel to Galway city to avail of many basic health care services. From the start, the project recognised that a basic health care problem was the conflict between the principles of efficiency and equity - efficiency suggesting that health services should be concentrated to provide economies of scale; and equity, which suggested that they should be as close to the client as possible. These arguments revolve around the additional costs of providing services locally (through the local Clifden hospital and through community services). The Health Board argues that it could provide, in Galway City, hospitals with the most advanced range of care possible. Residents point out that Galway is two hours distant and that once there, there may be a prolonged wait for treatment. The baseline study suggested that the need to travel to Galway to avail of basic health care was causing people to forego treatment. The study reported that women did not avail of ante-natal programmes until six months into pregnancy simply because they were only available in the city of Galway. Not only was it a long distance to the hospitals in Galway, but over 50% of the population was more than five miles from a doctor, nurse or chemist.

The Ballyconneely primary health care project explored some of these competing demands in one of the regions of the Forum project (its population is 800). The conclusions were that the delivery of health care in Connemara *should* be different from the national pattern. High out-migration in the young and middle-age groups means that there will be additional pressure on health services from elderly people, where problems of illness, disability and geriatric conditions are concentrated: on average, elderly people are three times more likely to need to attend a doctor monthly than people in younger age groups. However, most of the services they require are long-term, semi-skilled, low-technology and are best provided in the home. It recommended the use of non-emergency ambulances and community buses, day care services, and mobile day hospitals.

Forum proposed a number of ways of bringing health services closer to the people. In July 1993 it proposed to the Western Health Board that there be a day centre for elderly people in Clifden hospital, including a radiology service. Much of the debate on services concerns the small Clifden hospital, which has 30 beds (and 15 in another section which is closed). The hospital has no facilities for X-rays or blood testing. The Ballyconneely Health Group proposed that Clifden be upgraded to an emergency service, with X-ray facility, respite care and post-operative care.

9.1.3 Carers

With the local public health nurse, Forum carried out a study of carers. The sample was 39 carers, identified by the PHN. The main findings were that 42% of carers were over 61 and 44% of carers were men. 81% did not choose to become carers (a quarter had given up work to become carers). Two thirds spent over eight hours a day caring, twice the national level. 34% said that they never got a break; 25% felt they were unsupported in their role as carer. About a quarter of carers' dependants were disabled, incontinent, senile, or required intensive levels of support. Overall, carers experienced feelings of isolation, lack of recognition and financial loss. They required help in the area of information, skills training, emotional support (e.g. carers support group) and regular and sufficient respite care.

The report confirmed research already carried out into the needs of carers by the National Council for the Aged, but with some important local variations. The case for improved support for carers has already been recognised by the Department of Health (The years ahead - a policy for the elderly, Department of Health, 1988). Following the report, Forum took the decision to set up a carers support group to organise respite care for invalided elderly people as well as day care and sitting services.

9.2   Limerick City

9.2.1   Unemployment and health and housing exclusion

PAUL worked in urban housing estates where there is a concentration of *younger* age groups. In Moyross, one of PAUL's target areas, 57% of people are under 25 years of age, compared to the national average of 44%. Another important factor is that 26% of Moyross households renting from Limerick Corporation are headed by lone parents.

'Lack of community' has been one of the main criticisms of modern urban housing estates. These problems have been especially acute in Limerick, where estates have been characterised by a high turnover of residents, the out-migration of those in employment and a high percentage of low-income families.

In Moyross, for its 1,160 households, there is only one small shop and no public telephone, post office, pub, cafe, restaurant or library. There is also a poor infrastructure, lack of amenities, absence of employment opportunities, lack of structured activities for young people or a centre with which they could associate. Many young people expressed feelings of boredom, neglect, insecurity and isolation.

PAUL identified serious housing difficulties in another target area, Our Lady of Lourdes Parish. A number of elderly people, many of them owners, identified draughts, insufficient heating and dampness as major problems. Amongst local authority tenants, the level of dissatisfaction with the Corporation regarding maintenance is very high (94%). A numbar of tenants had taken out loans to ensure maintenance themselves. 14% of houses do not have a bathroom. One family in four had one member regularly requiring medical attention and there is a dearth of amenities for young and old, especially during the day.

9.2.2   Families under stress
Particular problems are faced by families in disadvantaged areas, as they struggle to raise young families without adequate social support. Lone parents are an especially vulnerable category (they account for 14% of all family units in the city and 24% in public housing areas). One acute consequence of their social isolation is having their child put into care.

PAUL established a lone parent network across the city, with membership of 40 parents. Two courses were run: 16 lone parents participated in counselling courses and 56 in personal development courses. Subsequently, the project pioneered a programme to integrate lone parents into the Labour market with EC Horizon funding. This programme highlights the considerable financial and institutional obstacles experienced by lone parents who wish to seek employment, and the project has made policy representations on getting these removed.

In 1989, 71% of children taken into care were from lone-parent families, emphasizing the vulnerability of these family units and the lack of support available to them elsewhere. The experience of having children taken into care is, says PAUL, a very traumatic one: most parents feel isolated and powerless in coping with the experience. Parents with children in care have no forum in which to come together to share experiences and to highlight the issues which concern them. The relationship between the State (through the Health Board) and the family regarding the care of children at risk is very unequal, the family having little control over decisions once the State becomes involved.

PAUL, with the support of the Mid-Western Health Board, also initiated a project to promote the rights of children who have families in care and to develop a support network for them. A hundred families with children in care were contacted, a core group of 10 to 15 families eventually being established. PAUL is preparing an information pack for families. A charter of rights for families was accepted by the Department of Health and an independent forum established for the families concerned. PAUL claims that the initiative has been of considerable help to the families, restoring personal confidence, and reducing feelings of isolation, guilt and shame.

9.3   Travellers
9.3.1   Exclusion from health and accommodation

DTEDG began to examine more systematically, and to make responses to, the health issues affecting Travellers in 1991. The initial response was the piloting of a Training Programme for Traveller Women in Primary Health Care. The earlier training programmes with Traveller women provided the catalyst for this because of the serious issues affecting the women participating in these programmes.

Next, with the support of the Combat Poverty Agency, DTEDG hired a researcher to establish and document the major health issues of Travellers, with a view to making recommendations to the Department of Health which had announced that it was formulating a National Health Strategy.

A written submission was made to the Department of Health (September 1993) which reviewed previous research on Irish Travellers' Health and also reviewed the relevant literature on social inequality and health status in relation to a number of minority ethnic groups. The submission also highlighted the relationship between Travellers' poor health and their living conditions and evaluated the role of the Health Boards in relation to Travellers.

Finally, the report made a series of recommendations covering living conditions, education, delivery of services, outreach work, research standards, positive action etc. on how the health situation of Travellers could be radically improved. In addition to the written submission, a delegation from DTEDG (Travellers and settled people) had a meeting with the Minister for Health, on 2nd December, 1993, to discuss the issues raised in the research.

9.3.2 'No place to go'

One of the key issues confronted by the DTEDG is the lack of suitable accommodation for Travellers. In Ireland, the local housing authorities have responsibility for meeting the accommodation needs of Travellers. In 1992, the Irish Travellers Movement, together with the DTEDG, published *No place to go - Travellers' accommodation in Dublin: report on a crisis situation* which was an attempt to measure accommodation needs and to put forward proposals for meeting them.

The report found that there were 606 Traveller families with 2,120 children under 15 in the greater Dublin area. It found that there were 27 official sites for 272 Traveller families, 31 unofficial sites for 208 Traveller families and a further nine temporary sites for 126 Traveller families. Looking at the families in more detail, 307 families had no toilet, 281 families had no water and 402 families had no electricity. There were no fire precautions on 50 sites.

The report commented: 'To live without a toilet, electricity or your own water supply in a capital city of a west European country in 1992 is beyond most people's comprehension, but it is a reality for most Travellers' (p 8). The report noted that many sites were infested with rats. One site is located beside a dump.

The report noted that the local authority had built a number of temporary sites in Dublin, but regarded them as unsatisfactory, being without individual electricity and surrounded by mounds of earth and dirt. It warned that the sites could well become permanent and that this was, in effect, a policy of building shanty towns on public money.

The report was critical of what it described as the 'snail's pace' of site provision. Over 1986-92, site provision had catered for only 16 families a year throughout the Dublin area. It conceded that, in some areas, there were objections by local residents, but it pointed out that in some areas, where there were no objections or legal or financial obstacles to the development of sites, progress had also been slow. Dun Laoghaire Corporation had no published plans for site accommodation at all: 'Their attitude over the years has been to attempt to deny all responsibility for site accommodation'. Endless delays are unacceptable and inexcusable, the report says: they reflect an attitude that Travellers' needs are not important. The report warns that the Traveller population is continuing to increase and that the rate of provision has made no attempt to account for future needs.

The report proposed that Traveller sites must include:
- workspace for Traveller economic activity and vans;
- individual flush toilets for each family;
- showers and baths separate from the toilet area; and
- sites not to be surrounded by high walls or mounds of earth.

The DTEDG invited local authority officials and councillors to attend a public meeting to see how the issues raised by the report could best be progressed (8 December 1992). The local authority administrative officer responsible for the development of Traveller sites in the County Council area said that Dublin County Council's sites for Travellers were superior to those in Britain and on the Continent and had received the highest praise. The much-criticised temporary sites were preferable to roadside halts. Regarding cooperation between voluntary organisations and the local authority, he said that voluntary organisations had a responsibility to teach Travellers about their responsibilities. Voluntary organisations had adopted an openly confrontational role. The administrative officer asked whether there was any point in dealing with the issues raised in the report. His council had taken an enlightened attitude toward Travellers: the report *No place to go* was an insult to Dublin County Council, his staff and to him personally. He then left the meeting. He did not refute the facts in the report.

This outcome raises a number of key issues in the Poverty 3 programme, one of which is the readiness of some public authorities to engage in dialogue on questions of social exclusion. Clearly, some bodies dealing with social exclusion in Ireland are not yet ready for such dialogue: notions of partnership between voluntary and statutory organisations are, presumably, a stage distant.

In an effort to improve the standard of halting sites, the DTEDG worked closely with the President in the establishment of the President Robinson Awards for Traveller Accommodation. This was an initiative of the President herself, who at a meeting of the project proposed awards for architects who designed a scheme for Traveller halting sites that would best meet Traveller needs. The underlying purpose was to introduce notions of quality into the design of Traveller accommodation that had hitherto been absent.

The competition encouraged many entries from architects and architectural students. One award winner spent several weeks with Travellers to familiarize himself with their needs and traditions. The DTEDG especially welcomed his entry for paying attention to nomadism, quality of materials, the integration of the workplace with accommodation, and attention to lighting, safety and playgrounds for children.

9.4 Policy issues

Lack of accommodation and the inadequacy of some existing housing remains a significant problem in Irish society. The squalid conditions facing Travellers are undisputed, and the fact that the response to their deprivation is lamentably short of what is required.

Health Boards in every region need to carry out and publish a health and safety statement on Traveller sites on a regular basis. This statement should cover such areas as: environmental health and safety issues, sanitary facilities, water supply, vermin control, overcrowding and pollution.

Procedures for applying for Medical Cards should be simplified and cards should be valid for a minimum period of five years for all doctors on the GMS list.

A Health Education Programme aimed specifically at Travellers' health concerns should be set up immediately. Positive action is required to give Travellers access to professional training as health care providers as well as the provision of a Primary Health Care Programme.

Forum highlighted the problem of poor quality rural housing. It provides compelling evidence that about one-eighth of the population live in conditions far below what is acceptable for a modern society. PAUL provides similar evidence in Limerick. The last official assessment of housing needs were carried out by the local authorities under s. 9 of the Housing Act, 1988, in March 1993. It found only 207 people living in unfit or unsuitable accommodation in the entire county of Galway and only 34 in Limerick city. The Forum and PAUL experience casts doubt on these figures as serious or in any way professional estimates of housing needs.

Declarations in the mid-1980s by Government and local authority housing officials that the housing problem in Ireland had been 'solved' fuelled complacency about the quality of housing in the country. Even with the expansion of the national housing programme in 1993, poor quality housing deserves a more prominent place on the agenda of social exclusion programmes.

Turning to health and personal social services, the PAUL project provides a classic example of the way in which a local model action can pioneer a service for a particular social need, in this case, the families of children in care. PAUL identified this need, small in size but nonetheless real, and provided an appropriate, comprehensive range of services in a relatively short period of time, bringing an excluded and unpopular group into the mainstream of the health service network. It has extended this work into the economic realm also, by developing a programme which specifically promotes education, training and employment opportunities for lone parents.

Forum raises a fundamental question as to how health service delivery may be made more appropriate in a remote region and states unambiguously that inappropriate or inaccessible services contribute to social exclusion. Its thesis that health services must adapt to problems of distance is well made and shows that 'proximity of services' is a real issue. Additional strength to its approach is given by its research findings that the need of remote areas is for properly-funded, low-tech, long-term, semi-skilled, community-delivered services. Forum's own provision of resource centres for the elderly, of support services for carers and of improved communications for isolated people, shows how health services can be delivered locally and appropriately, in a relatively short period of time and at relatively low cost. It demonstrates that good services can be delivered to a dispersed, depleted population. Forum's case and track record deserve a comprehensive response from the health authorities, not only in Ireland, but further afield.

CHAPTER 10

Local development and social exclusion

An important function of socially inclusive policies is to overcome the cumulative disadvantage which communities face through geographical isolation, poor planning and inadequate local government structures. A number of local strategies were devised to overcome problems of exclusion in the two areas served by the model action projects.

10.1   North-west Connemara
10.1.1   Rural exclusion
NW Connemara suffers problems of exclusion associated with its remoteness. The distance to the county capital, Galway, is 80km, but the problem of distance is made worse by poor infrastructure. The only railway in the area, the line to Clifden, was withdrawn in 1935. Roads deteriorated due to lack of resources for maintenance. Public bus services declined. The nearest general hospital is Galway. The local authority is also based there and although the County Council has an office in Clifden, it serves only as a base for the authority's engineer. In Connemara, 37% of the population belong to a household without a car, compared to the national average of 22%.

Distance from services is an inevitable aspect of living in remote rural districts. Some areas are quite outlying. 8% of people are more than 8km from a bus route; 13% are more than 8km from a primary school. Over three-quarters of residents are within 8km of a shop, post office or telephone, but distances from doctors, dentists and chemists are much further.

Despite these difficulties, community activities are highly organized in Connemara. The baseline study found that about 49% of people participated in local groups or organisations. A total of 62 voluntary organisations were identified in the area, comprising support and advice groups, welfare organisations, education groups, leisure and sports clubs, political parties, religious groups and groups dedicated to community, economic or enterprise development. Most had been established in the last 10 years; most had a core of five to six active members. Only 17% receive State grants or similar support. The main difficulties these groups experience are lack of financial resources, lack of local facilities and amenities and transport difficulties in organising events.

10.1.2   Transport
Transport was an important focus of the work of Forum. North and west Connemara is an area of extremely low population density - 9/km² compared

to 51/km² in the rest of Ireland and 143/km² in the EU as a whole. The project includes the only island in the Irish Poverty 3 programme - Inishbofin (219 people). Transport was repeatedly raised by people in the area as a serious obstacle to personal contact, access to health and social services, community development, and meeting basic economic needs.

In the absence of any State initiatives to improve transport services, the project coordinated the establishment of four new transport routes, the first of which opened in December 1991. Three of the services offered:
- twice daily service, Clifden to Westport (summer only);
- weekly Connemara intervillage service (Ballyconneely, Roundstone and Clifden); and
- weekly service from Inishbofin to Clifden and Galway, timed with the boat service.

These services were run by a privately-owned bus but, on Inishbofin island, a community landrover service was introduced which also functioned as an ambulance. The Department of Social Welfare was asked to approve bus passes on these routes and in July 1993 agreed to do so. The project's contribution was staff time, administration, publicity and technical advice. In the case of the Inishbofin service, the project gave a contribution of £3,000, to match £7,000 which the islanders raised themselves. The bus is operated by a rota of volunteer drivers.

The project made a proposal to the Department of Transport to fund a three-year, £154,100 pilot transport scheme to develop new routes. It suggested that the pilot scheme be operated by a partnership committee comprising Forum, the Department of Transport, the Department of Social Welfare, Bus Éireann, the Western Health Board, An Post, Galway County Council, and the private sector. Eventually, in the Government's 1994 budget, £30,000 was allocated to Forum to undertake a pilot transport project in NW Connemara.

10.1.3 Community development
Building the capacity of the local communities was an important aspect of the work of both model actions in their attempts to overcome exclusion. In Connemara, Forum invested considerable effort to improve the ability of the local communities to plan for their own future. Its initial work concentrated on three existing groups: the Recess development group; Cleggan and Claddaduff community council and Clifden & District community council.

Forum offered weekly meetings designed to enhance the groups' abilities in lobbying, in dealing with local government, in funding and in developing legal structures. Most of the work of the community groups focused on the development of a local community facility. As a result of its efforts, Recess is now developing a school as a community centre; Cleggan is planning a resource centre for the elderly. Seventeen members of these groups attended a community development course in University College Galway. Forum also made grants available to ten community development organisations for planning, first aid, amenity development and cheese-making courses.

Hitherto women have been underrepresented in development groups and community councils. Forum ran three FÁS-funded community development and enterprise courses for 20, 23 and 24 women respectively. These courses were oversubscribed, 52 applying for the last course. Training was provided in social analysis, assertiveness, group skills and enterprise development. Forum reported that women are now more involved in community development, that participation rates of women rose and that there were considerable gains in personal development. As a result of one course, a number of women set up a home-produce and bakery business.

Forum paid for the creche service which facilitated women to participate in the course. FÁS does not fund creche facilities for its training programmes. Forum points out that for many women, participation in the course would be impossible without such facilities. Forum worked with six women's groups - in Letterfrack, Renvyle, Inishbofin, Clifden and Roundstone. Some are support groups, others craft groups.

10.2   Limerick City
10.2.1   Social exclusion in the urban context
It is recently recognised that social exclusion takes on a distinct form in urban areas and Limerick city is a prime example of this. PAUL identifies four issues of concern:

i. The concentration of the unemployed and other low income households in local authority housing areas, which are themselves geographically centred in the inner core of the city. The socio-economic profile of Limerick Corporation tenants reveals that 86% depend principally on social welfare, with 32% in receipt of an unemployment payment. Indeed, almost half of the unemployed in Limerick live in an area which contains a quarter of the city's population.

ii. The poor quality of public and private services available in public housing estates in terms of recreational amenities, difficulties in accessing jobs, shopping, credit and other facilities, together with inadequate maintenance of houses and estates. Moyross for instance, a community of 5,000 people, has three small grocery shops, no public phones, no chemist and no resident doctor. Inadequate services are compounded by vandalism, social and political alienation, further lowering the quality of life on these estates.

iii. The social stigma and 'bad press' which is attached to those areas with high levels of unemployment. This negative image is a major problem within Limerick city and indeed characterises the entire city at a national level. Estates, and the people who live in them, get reputations and images which have the effect of compounding existing patterns of exclusion. This can pose immediate difficulties for residents seeking jobs and other services and also undermines the residential stability of the population as existing residents move to more 'desirable areas'.

iv. The lack of community support structures in the newer public housing estates, especially those such as pre-school classes, information outlets, recreational facilities and voluntary organisations. In some areas, such as Southill, the existing infrastructure was undermined by the population exodus caused by the £5,000 housing surrender grant.

10.2.2 Estate management

In March 1993, the Department of the Environment circulated a memorandum on housing management to all local housing authorities, including Limerick Corporation. This requested each local authority to submit a written statement of how it proposed to improve the management of its housing stock. The Department stressed that the needs, wishes and aspirations of tenants must be taken into account; the participation of tenants in the running of estates was inadequate and insufficiently encouraged. Estate maintenance must be improved in quality and made programmatic rather than response-orientated.

A seminar to review the memorandum was organized by PAUL together with one of its partners, Limerick Corporation, to which residents of local authority estates and public representatives were invited. According to PAUL, the memorandum provided an opportunity to develop a systematic and planned approach to the management of housing estates. As a result of

the seminar, PAUL made a number of proposals for estate management based on the following principles:
- a positive acknowledgement of the role of tenants in estate management;
- an election process giving all tenants the chance to participate;
- technical assistance for estate management groups;
- facilitation of groups to network with other estate management groups locally and nationally;
- systems for involving tenant-purchasers in matters affecting them;
- a systematic maintenance programme;
- user-friendly rent collection methods, with provision for people in arrears; and
- training for Corporation staff in customer care and relations.

PAUL initiated the first tenant estate management group in Limerick in 1993 in O'Malley Park. The O'Malley Park estate management group has already drawn up plans for the refurbishment of the park. PAUL stressed the importance of there being an integrated urban development plan for each area on a five-yearly basis, one that would recognize the community's role in policy formulation and planning.

10.3   Policy issues
The work of the three Irish projects suggests that strategies against social exclusion must be based on broad concepts of the dimensions of exclusion. This chapter shows how exclusion touches on wider questions such as urban and rural development policies.

PAUL's research raises serious questions concerning the type of projects supported in urban renewal strategies. It is very clear from PAUL that there are serious problems in the physical environment, amenities and facilities in low-income local authority housing areas in the city. Despite that, the amount allocated to improving the physical infrastructure of disadvantaged estates is still small compared to the urban renewal programme operated in the city. By 1992, £106m had been allocated to the programme, including King John's Castle and two quayside projects. The concentration of resources on these projects, at a time when there are such pressing demands for improving the lived environment in low income housing estates, must be questioned.

The partnership model illustrates an alternative approach to urban development, one which enjoins social and economic objectives, mobilises state, social and community agencies and gives a key role to the intended beneficiaries.

The tenant estate management project organized by PAUL, in conjunction with Limerick Corporation, at last brings Ireland into line with continental European practices of estate management. Such work is still at a primitive stage of development in Ireland: continental European practices have moved on to the use of concierge systems and unobtrusive, high-tech estate security.

Forum's work in the transport field exposes the continuing inability of the Department of Transport to organise a transport policy for remote rural areas. Long after our European neighbours discovered the virtues of coordinated and integrated transport policies in physical environments more challenging than ours, it is baffling that in Ireland, rural transport continues to be gridlocked between seven different Government agencies and departments.

In the Poverty 3 programme, it is notable that Forum had both the scope and the resources to tackle this particular aspect of social exclusion and was able to make new bus routes operational. The coordination value of model action projects may well be more important than has been realised.

A further noteworthy feature of the Connemara bus routes is their low cost. Apart from Forum's coordination role and the Department of Social Welfare's subsidy of bus passes, these bus routes have cost no direct public money. Indeed, they are run at operational profit, suggesting that the costs of bridging communication problems in rural areas may be much less than have been thought.

Related to the developments in transport and tourism is the community development work of Forum. The project has given attention to building up the capacity of the local community to plan its own future, developing not just personal, but community skills. Democratic planning of tourism and transport presupposes a firm community infrastructure. Forum's community development work has already yielded positive results and the FÁS-funded courses have done much to strengthen the participation of women in the community and social process. Indeed, FÁS's support for this programme shows the degree to which the national approach to community training has moved beyond the 1970s-derived, urban-orientated models, to new ones of 'training for citizenship'. This work, and that done by PAUL, reinforces the importance of community-building in model action projects, of anti-poverty programmes and of giving a voice and cohesion to hitherto silent and neglected areas.

CHAPTER 11

PAUL Partnership

CLEAR GRE[]

SAVE

BOTTLE & AL[]

CAN B[]

2292[]

TEL. 061- 229232

**BOTTLE BANK
& ALUMINIUM CANS**

NO PARKING
NO RESPONSIBILITY
TAKEN FOR LOSS
OR DAMAGE TO
ARTICLES OR VEHICLES

BROWN

SAVE IT
BOTTLE &
ALUMINIUM CAN
BANK 229232

NIUM

SAVE IT
BOTTLE &
ALUMINIUM C
BANK 22923

101

PAUL
PARTNERS
LIMERICK

tide of un

geal gloine

Hand Crafted Items
in Stained Glass
including
Light Catchers

Studio 30,
Workspace,
Michael Stre
Limerick

Organisational responses to social exclusion

The working methods of the Irish Poverty 3 projects represented a new organisational model to counterbalance sectorally-based national development models. These elements were: an area focus, targeting of least privileged groups, multidimensionality, partnership and participation. Other themes are those of networking to exchange best practice, and policy experimentation to chart new directions in Government thinking. How this model was implemented in reponding to social exclusion is the theme of this chapter.

12.1   Partnership: the experience of the two model action projects

The partnership models which operated in the Poverty 3 programme were among the main innovations. It is important to note that there were two distinct styles in the Irish project: highly structured partnerships with the State and local authorities (the model actions) and flexible forms of partnerships (DTEDG). Many other forms of partnership could be found within the Poverty 3 programme in Europe as a whole, of which these were only two of up to six distinct approaches.

The two model actions have a positive sense of their experience of partnership, the general perception being that their type of partnership has worked well. Moreover, there is evidence that this type of model inspired the forms of partnership which developed in the years following the setting up of the projects - such as the PESP companies (1991) and the County Enterprise Boards (1993).

The model actions believe that the main gains from the partnership experience have been:
• in efficiency;
• in closer access to decision-making; and
• as a bridge between the culture of the voluntary sector and the State.

12.1.1   Efficiency gains

Projects claim that there are efficiency gains from these partnership models. PAUL's money advice project, for example, benefited from the participation on its board of the Mid-western Health Board, the Department of Social Welfare and Limerick Corporation. Whilst all might have cooperated in any case, their membership of the board committed them to representatives working on a problem raised by the project and reduced the need of the project to persuade these bodies separately. The partnership mechanism saved the project considerable time and energy.

The model action projects are positive about partnership as a way of widening the range of information available to projects, 'giving local people the broad picture' and in spreading knowledge about the work of State agencies.

12.1.2   Closer access to decision-makers

There are ways in which the partnership mechanism provided greater access to decision-making channels and widened a project's circle of contacts.   A particular case in point is where a community and enterprise course proposed by Forum to FÁS was delayed. Forum requested the intervention of the FÁS member of the Forum board.   What followed is recorded by Forum:

> The uncertainty which surrounded the course was most undesirable. If [the FÁS member of the board] had not taken up our case we would have had to cancel the course, or at the very least, postpone it until FÁS would release funds at a national level.   Without his help, we would still be waiting to know the fate of the course.   This proves the point that partnership can be dependent, to a great extent, on the goodwill of managers of statutory bodies.   [He] is most enthusiastic about the course but without his enthusiasm it is probable that we would not have had a second course (Forde, 1993).

Thus partnership provides a welcome additional weapon in the system of political pressure and clientelism that characterizes the Irish administrative system.

12.1.3   A bridge between the culture of the voluntary sector and the State

The general requirement by the Department of the Environment that local authorities undertake estate management schemes led to a visit by PAUL staff to Liverpool, England, to observe practices there.   Participants on the visit included staff, community delegates, Limerick Corporation housing officers and public representatives.   The visit smoothed the way for the PAUL proposal and its subsequent adoption, meaning that cooperation on such joint projects is more likely in the future.   It is an important part of the building of trust between the voluntary and statutory sector.   Partnership thus provided an opportunity for voluntary sector and state sector representatives to work closely together.   Personnel in the model actions emphasized the term 'building of trust' on numerous occasions.   Indeed, the partnership experience in the model actions has generated much enthusiasm, even heady rhetoric.   This is worth probing.   Two explanations are offered.

First, the model action partnership design may fill the gap in Irish local government. Local government in Ireland is weak in comparison to that of its European neighbours and is poorly resourced in terms of planning, research or consultation. Its structure and functions have changed little since its introduction in 1898. It is not development-orientated and has grave difficulties in operating in a social development context or in cooperating with voluntary organisations. In distant rural areas, it is considered to be remote and not sensitive to local needs. It is possible that a partnership model may provide an opportunity for state authorities to cooperate and function together, which in other countries would normally be accommodated through the channels of local government. Indeed, Forum at one stage proposed that its partnership model be the basis for a new and more responsive sub-county structure of local government.

Second, divisions between the culture of the voluntary sector and the State may be wider than in other European countries. Partly reflecting recruitment patterns, there is very little traffic in personnel between the two, few people moving from the State to work in the voluntary sector or vice versa. The staff of voluntary organisations tend to be younger than their statutory partners; they may well be female while the statutory personnel they deal with are male. There is little shared in-service training, common professional associations or common organs of communication between the two. Accordingly, the partnership mechanism may represent the first attempt to bridge these large deficits of experience, background and communication.

However, the model actions are clear that partnership did not work equally well with all their statutory partners. The level of commitment, of time and of energies to partnership seems to have varied. Partnership appears to work best with agencies which have a developmental approach to their work. Forum, for example, developed a positive relationship with BIM, which was looking for a local agency through which it could develop its aquaculture activities. BIM is based in Dublin and does not have the resources to build up a strong regional presence. BIM noted:

> Forum has been a learning experience for us at BIM. We must take increasing account of local conditions and human and social factors in our development programme. We are now trying to emulate the Forum experience by appointing local development officers in four other coastal regions with the support of the LEADER/INTERREG programmes (Forum News, June 1993, p 5).

Not only did BIM provide a local development worker, but it generated some enthusiasm for the aquaculture business. Likewise, the Mid-Western Health Board, in developing its work with the families of children in care, delivered this new service through PAUL. PAUL was the 'legitimizer' of a State service. Both these partners put cash, as well as time and effort, into the project.

But the converse seems also to have been true. Forum's relationship with Galway County Council was limited. The County Council partner could not meet local demands for improved infrastructure. However, other partnership structures were not fully explored by the County Council, for example, local consultative structures. The degree to which other partners changed their approaches or 'mainstreamed' ideas learned from model actions is clearly difficult to assess. Evidence of mainstreaming is not yet evident from most of the partners.

Whilst this section is primarily a discussion on the experiences of the model actions, some of the limits to partnership were felt sharply in the Dublin Travellers project when it presented its report on Traveller accommodation in the Dublin area, which, as we have seen, met with strong denunciation by the County Council. Despite the gains from partnership, it is clear that as a process it can be slow, difficult and time-consuming. It will produce agreement on some issues, but cannot be expected to do so on all.

12.2   The right partners?

A question which must be addressed at this stage is whether the partnerships were either wide enough, or appropriate enough, to promote the issues raised by the projects. The question of entering partnership with non-developmental type partners has already been raised. But in addition, both model actions addressed important aspects of policy in the absence of partnership with the appropriate Government departments. The most obvious examples are in education (PAUL) and tourism and transport (Forum). Although the projects may not have anticipated the importance of these subjects when they began their work, there might have been considerable benefit had the projects been able to draw in the appropriate authorities (namely the Departments of Education, Tourism and Transport respectively). Forum involved the Industrial Development Authority (IDA) and Bord Fáilte in its subcommittees, but not as full partners. Forum invited the Department of Education to be a project partner but was told that the Department did not have the legal authority to enter such an arrangement.

It is a matter of speculation whether more progress might have been made on these points had these lead-Departments been involved from the start. Although PAUL included Shannon Development, the participation of State agencies for industrial development was weak. Future projects may wish to consider new development agencies Forfás and Forbairt. Likewise, if future urban projects dealing with social exclusion confront questions of crime and transport for example, the involvement of the law enforcement and urban transport bodies will be essential.

A category strikingly absent from the partnership of the model actions was elected local authority councillors. This marked the Irish partnerships as quite different from their continental European counterparts, most of which involved councillors or the local mayor. A possible future approach might be for local authorities to express their partnership role through adoption of a formal resolution of the council concerned.

Equally, on the non-governmental side, it is important to ask whether all the appropriate partners were present. PAUL, for example, did not include groups working with the Travellers in the city in its partnership, even though there are a considerable number of Travellers in Limerick.

Some model actions seem to have struggled with the presence of some partners. PAUL, for example, as part of the ABR, found it difficult to identify a role for and a benefit from the trade union and employer representatives. It is possible that the passive support and political acquiescence of some of the social partners is a necessary aspect of partnership, but future projects will need to be clearer about the roles of active and passive partner members.

12.3 The experience of partnership in the innovative project

Like other innovative projects in Poverty 3, the DTEDG did not adopt a partnership approach on the line of the model actions. From the start it stated that it wished to choose partners as needs and circumstances arose. Had it been part of a more formal, structured arrangement, it felt that its style, freshness and ability to respond, at short notice, to situations facing its target group would have been severely curbed. It valued its freedom to operate as a small, independent project. An important function of anti-poverty projects must be to challenge mainstream economic and political structures. In its Interim Report to the Poverty 3 Programme, DTEDG elaborated on this theme:

Area-based model action type projects cannot be presumed to give adequate attention to the specific needs of such marginalized groups as Travellers or Gypsies. In setting priorities there may be a tendency to relegate the most despised sectors to the lowest rung of the hierarchy of needs. Policies and practices tend to exclude the most marginalized groups unless they explicitly set out to include them and introduce affirmative action to do so.

There is more than one model of partnership. Poverty 3 has tended to focus almost exclusively on the institutional management committee model. Models should be tested and developed, which may require more dynamic and flexible structures. There is a need for variety and experiment in relation to these models at national and EC level.

DTEDG warned against rushing headlong into 'partnership' simply because it is a word with warm, positive, consensual connotations. Partnership may well bring influence, but at a very high price for the organisation and the people it works with. It pointed out that as far back as 1963, the *Commission on Itinerancy* identified the importance of the State working in partnership with voluntary organisations, such as the voluntary itinerant settlement committees. Such a partnership was used by the State to justify the assimilationist strategy which it defined. Voluntary organisations legitimized this inappropriate and unsuccessful strategy. Work against social exclusion must also be about dissent and different perspectives.

The approach of DTEDG to partnership seems to have been vindicated. First, there is firm evidence that a number of State and local authorities are not yet willing to enter dialogue, still less partnership with Traveller organisations. The confrontational approach of Dublin County Council is one example. The Department of Education, as seen by its approach to the National Education Convention, does not yet seem ready for dialogue with some socially excluded groups. Indeed, its approach to dialogue seems to be to reinforce the existing hierarchy of powerful interest groups in the area of educational politics.

Second, the value of the *ad hoc* approach is evident if one examines the unusual list of participants in the partnership around the President Robinson Award Scheme, which comprised Travellers, Government departments north and south, professional associations (e.g. architects) and local authorities. The President herself described it as a partnership which was 'a blueprint for a better understanding, for an imaginative and exciting dialogue'.

Third, DTEDG was able to win some 'seats at the table' and political influence *without* a formal partnership arrangement. For example, two representatives of the project participate on the Dublin County Council Committee on Traveller Settlement and have made presentations to the committee. DTEDG was invited to fill two places on the Task Force on the Travelling Community, set up in 1993. To DTEDG, these are examples of flexible working which permit influence *without* compromise.

12.4   Participation

One of the key principles of the Poverty 3 programme was the participation of those targeted by the programme. Initially, such participation was structured on a representative basis at board level. Later, the projects used additional methods to broaden participation. In PAUL this was achieved through subcommittees, programme development workshops and its community action centres. In Forum, participation was implemented through its executive committee, subcommittees and programme working groups. Travellers participated in all the subcommittees of the DTEDG project and took part in delegations speaking to politicians or public meetings.

The projects observed that participation in the projects as they were constructed requires high levels of self-confidence and technical skills. The technical skills for taking part in projects at the formal decision-making stage are of at least graduate level. The documentation which the projects received from the agencies to which they were accountable required familiarity with social and political concepts, documentation and accountancy. All the projects took the decision to invest in efforts to raise the educational and training level of the target groups so that they might more effectively participate in the operation of the project.

The three Irish projects all consider participation to be a worthy principle of the programme. However, more thought is required as to how it may best be operationalized, especially the training and educational investments necessary to make it meaningful. This should be given early attention in the next round of projects against social exclusion.

12.5 The experimental nature of the programme

It has already been emphasized that the three Irish Poverty 3 projects are experimental, demonstration projects. The three projects were opportunities to test approaches to particular social problems. The piloting approach has been an innovation in Irish social policy since the Second Poverty Programme when a number of pilot projects became the basis for the Community Development Programme (established 1990) and the grant scheme for locally based women's groups.

PAUL was the testing ground for three particular experiments: ABRs, the Horizon project for lone parents and the Indebtedness Scheme. The ABR were successful to the point that in February, 1994, the Government announced that under the *National Plan, 1994-9* the ABR approach would be extended to 33 areas at a cost of £100m. The same month, the Minister for Social Welfare announced that the Indebtedness Scheme Pilot Project had been so successful that it would be extended forthwith to eight new areas and expanded to a three-year programme. In other areas, the BIM approach to aquaculture in Forum was subsequently applied in LEADER projects. Forum's pioneering work in rural transport services has now led to a £30,000 pilot project, which, although small-scale, may lead in time to more ambitious schemes.

The presence of a locally-based partnership in a rural area such as NW Connemara, with its dispersed offices and staff, allows for effective and coordinated responses to local difficulties. But, as evidenced by Forum's work in aquaculture and housing for the elderly, such responses are not yet possible within the existing local authority structure.

In its piloting function the Poverty 3 programme had a clear impact. It provided a low-cost means of testing new approaches to social questions in a country where innovation has not yet been a prominent feature of social policy. But making such piloting effective in the future does raise the question as to how well these models of good practice become widely known and promoted through the public service and the channels of communication and training that must underpin the dissemination of such models.

12.6 Networking

All the projects took part in activities with other projects in the Poverty 3 programme; indeed, 5% of the total budget of each project was set aside for networking activities. For example, PAUL took part in transnational exchanges with the model action projects in Hamburg, Utrecht and Edinburgh. DTEDG attended a hearing on the situation of Gypsy and Traveller groups in Europe, held in Brussels in May 1991, initiated by President Delors.

Forum established close contacts with model action projects in Samiko, Denmark; Bucaneve, Italy; Bourgos, Spain; and Almeida and Beira, Portugal. They found much in common with models of rural development and tourism. Its representatives visited a fish farm in Brittany and studied rural development in Lapland. Forum commented on its transnational contacts with two model action projects in Portugal, which it found faced similar problems of unemployment, out-migration, underemployment, low agricultural incomes, illiteracy, poor housing and the difficulty of ensuring that local communities benefited from tourism. Forum observed how the subsidies and headage payments of the Common Agricultural Policy had made little impact either in Connemara or in the mountainous regions of Portugal:

> This is a common concern that can be tackled together. To become recognised lobbyists, peripheral communities have got to know and understand each other. Interproject visits have an important part to play in building effective networks and alliances (Chris Curtin, quoted in Visit to Portugal, Forum News, issue no.1, October 1991, p 9)

Likewise, DTEDG believes that its community work participative approach to working with Travellers is a model which is widely applicable throughout Europe and which should be used by future projects against poverty and social exclusion.

12.7   Concluding remarks
The three Irish Poverty 3 projects illustrate two models of partnership operating in the programme. DTEDG makes a strong case that other models should also be considered. They all demonstrate the principle of piloting initiatives that may then be adapted nationally.

In future programmes, questions must be raised about the appropriateness of partners. The Poverty 3 experience suggests that some key partners were absent (e.g. Education, Transport, Tourism, local authority councillors) and that others should be considered in future projects (e.g. police, industrial development agencies). Some existing partners may not be necessary. A vital first phase of any project is the process of exploring, establishing and agreeing levels of commitment of partners.

The Poverty 3 experience is clear that partnership worked best with development-orientated partners but leaves us with a question as to how future partnerships should address State authorities and agencies which do not have a developmental role. A final question left open by the programme is that of mainstreaming. At this stage we do not know enough about the degree to which lessons which partners learned in local projects have been reported back, and streamed into, the agencies concerned. We know very little about how and to what extent lessons learned at local level are applied nationally throughout participating agencies and about the information structure required to make this possible. A system of monitoring this process should be an important part of the next programme.

Implications for policy and action

This section brings together some of the key policy and organisational issues which have arisen in the course of the Poverty 3 programme in Ireland. It summarises those areas where the programme has made the most impact.

13.1   New insights on and responses to social exclusion

Forum restates the problem which in Ireland has been termed 'western decline' but which we now see as part of the wider problem of the declining peripheral rural areas of the European Union. In re-emphasizing the fragility of this peripheral economy, it draws attention to a number of ways in which the quality of life in these areas may be improved, especially through the more appropriate delivery of health and education services, the availability of transport and housing repair. Moreover, it has identified ways in which the peripheral economy may be improved through changes in tourism investment patterns and approaches. It identifies a number of tools, such as community development adult education and radio, which may build up the capacities of small, remote communities to effect change. The same possibilities also apply to other peripheral regions of the Union, such as Portugal, Spain and Greece.

PAUL's work underlines how the urban problems of Limerick fit not only the national Irish problem of urban decline, but the European one as well. It demonstrates how a combination of poor planning practices, ill-considered housing policies and unequal educational opportunities are exacerbated by rapid and negative changes in the labour market. Meanwhile, the response of the State authorities to those changes have been neither fast nor imaginative enough. PAUL's experience challenges Ireland to view itself as an urbanised society, as well as a rural and provincial one, and to adopt an integrated range of urban developmental policies. In doing so, PAUL isolates the elements for such an urban policy: local estate management, adult education, legitimisation of the shadow economy, self-employment, small and medium-size enterprises, investment in the physical structure and consumer-sensitivity of welfare services.

The DTEDG project has begun to effect a significant shift in the manner in which Travellers are perceived in Ireland. Its impact is most evident at national policy level. From being perceived as an anomalous 'problem group', Travellers are increasingly seen as a distinct cultural entity entitled to respect, recognition and full citizenship. The manner in which Travellers have been excluded from their citizenship has been identified as a form of racism. DTEDG has affirmed the crucial importance of effective legal protection for minorities and how such protection may be an important mechanism in combating exclusion throughout Europe, where Travellers and Gypsies face similar problems.

The work of the projects in the areas of unemployment, Social Welfare and education substantiates the important links between social exclusion and joblessness, welfare dependency and educational inequality and disadvantage. Unemployment problems may intensify as the Single Market is completed, and on foot of international agreements such as GATT which may bring further capital relocation. PAUL, in particular, confirms how local trends are influenced by national and international processes.

The programme has made an impact by introducing new policy issues which had not received prominence in the debate on social exclusion. The most important of these are the operation of social employment schemes, debt, transport, tourism, the quality of delivery of health services, radio, recycling and the role of racism. The projects confirm that poor accommodation and housing remain important public policy issues. The commitment to multidimensionality has encouraged social exclusion to be seen in a much wider framework, bringing in hitherto unexpected elements.

13.2   Broad questions raised by the projects

The three projects have two particular elements in common, both of which reflect on national and European anti-poverty policies. First, all the projects operate in a defined economic context and have a fundamental economic dimension. Combating social exclusion is not simply a question of social policy but has to do with a range of policies, especially economic policy. Whilst the links between economic and social policy have been broadly accepted for many generations in continental Europe, this has not always been the case in Ireland. In the debate on the first round of the structural funds, the Government view was that the funds should be 'economic' but that 'social' questions were an entirely separate concern. The research and action of the three Irish projects demonstrate once again the inseparability of these issues.

In NW Connemara, Forum demonstrates how the combating of social exclusion requires the development of appropriate short, medium and long-term economic activities in the areas of aquaculture and tourism. PAUL demonstrates the potential of self-employment and community businesses in areas of considerable deprivation. DTEDG illustrates how the Traveller community already plays a part in the recycling economy and outlined how it could play a much bigger role, granted the appropriate policies and support. The projects show clearly how, even in a difficult national and European labour market, there are distinct possibilities for economic development and economic routes out of poverty. These possibilities should be reflected in overall national and European policies for economic growth and development - in Ireland through State economic development policies, and in Europe through the White Paper on growth (1993) and the White Paper on social policy (forthcoming).

The three projects outline how public investment decisions operate in an exclusionary way. Forum demonstrates how the IRTC operated to favour commercial county radio interests in preference to local community interests. Forum shows how current tourism and aquaculture investment is directed to large-scale projects, and how existing barriers of finance and capital exclude people with little capital. PAUL has contrasted the lack of investment in working class estates with the tax incentives available for renewal of the urban fabric in commercial parts of the city. The model action projects also illustrate the extremely low levels of investment in adult education compared to conventional primary, secondary and third-level education; Forum questioned the investment in fixed-plant distant health services in preference to locally-delivered community services. Irish public investment has a choice in investment decisions and may decide the relative proportions between the two. The poverty projects state that these investment decisions have neither been equitable nor effective.

13.3   The impact of the projects

The size of the model action projects and their duration of funding have meant not only stability but also the possibility of drawing into the programme a wider range of people and communities. For example, PAUL was able to involve four parishes in Limerick and Forum nine distinct local communities. In the latter case, the nine communities began increasingly to see north and west Connemara as a distinct economic unit. The model actions widened the geographical scope of anti-poverty action compared to the Second Programme: Poverty 3 enlarged the range of services and activities in anti-poverty work. Few voluntary organisations hitherto had the opportunity to provide such a wide range of frontline services but they proved themselves well equal to the challenge. Forum states that over 100 people were directly involved in the project, and up to 4,000 benefited either directly or indirectly. This should give the Commission additional confidence in the preparation of a Fourth Poverty Programme and new Community Initiative Programmes. Local development projects like those of the Poverty 3 programme have demonstrated a positive impact far out of proportion to their size.

Poverty 3 is the only European programme dealing exclusively with poverty. The experience of the Poverty 3 projects in Ireland suggests that its approaches of targeting, partnership and multidimensionality could usefully be applied to other EU specialised programmes.

13.4   Research questions raised by the projects

Several research issues arose in the course of the Irish Poverty 3 projects. The first is to affirm the value of the research which was carried out. Several studies should be highlighted. The PAUL report on the costs of education was an original study shedding light on an area of public policy which hitherto had been poorly examined. The PAUL study on the Social Employment Scheme undoubtedly played a part in influencing the eventual Government decision to replace SES with Community Employment in January 1994. The PAUL report on debt also influenced the shape and detail of the Consumer Credit Bill, 1994, which proposes to regulate and restrict money-lending. The DTEDG study on the Traveller economy linked a frontier area of economic development - waste recycling - with a particular community's economic life which had hitherto been virtually undocumented. Forum's baseline study is one of the most comprehensive, thorough and wide-ranging local analyses of its kind. The Poverty 3 programme gave these projects the space, the opportunity and the resources to carry out these important and original research tasks.

Equally, it is important to highlight the problems which arise from the lack of research. This seems to have been a particular problem for the PAUL project, which was unable to complete its baseline study in the definition phase of the programme. The lesson here is that more time should be given to projects in the establishment phase to conduct basic research areas. In 1991 the Forum evaluator wrote:

> The model action projects of Poverty 3 can be said to share many of
> the characteristics of the Third World integrated rural development

projects. Studies of the latter show that they have had multiple, vague, often unrealistic and at times contradictory objectives. Incomes were to be raised, the poorest to be reached, women's concerns reflected, ecological balance maintained and people made participants in decision-making and implementation of project activities. This overload failed to give a clear aim to the projects and often demanded the impossible of project management and staff (Chris Curtin, *Forum Discussion Document*, January 1991).

The baseline report of Forum identified key target groups and areas of work for the project (e.g. the elderly, women, underemployed and unemployed) and based on that analysis, the work of the project was concentrated and overload avoided.

Forum found a remarkable level of community organisation; other studies in new urban areas indicate this is not just a rural phenomenon.

Forum

Published reports

Anne Byrne: *Baseline study*. Forum, 1991, 155 pp + app.

Michael Laver et al: *The delivery of health care services in north and west Connemara*. Forum, June 1992, 26 pp

Dr Mary Tubridy: *A plan for community-led sustainable tourism in north-west Connemara, 1994-97*. Forum, April 1993, in three vols.

Tom Lavin: *Partnership - the Forum experience. Rural development school*, RTE, 1992.

Anne Byrne: *Working for the health of rural women*. In Prof. Cecily Kelleher (Ed) *The future for health promotion*.

Mary Ruddy: *A summary of tourism development plan and launch proceedings, September 1993*. 41 pp + app.

Forum: *Plan of work 1992-94*. March 1992, 22 pp.

Submissions and policy documents

Brigid Quirke: *A primary health care proposal for north and west Connemara in partnership between the Western Health Board and Forum*. Forum, March 1992, 16 pp.

Forum: *Submission from Forum to the Department of Agriculture for an agricultural, tourism and environment programme*. Forum, 4 September 1992, 4 pp.

Forum: *Submission to the green paper on education*. Forum, 1992.

Connemara west: *Application to the Independent Radio and Television Commission*. 1993, 16 pp + app.

Forum: *Proposal for a study on the merits of establishing a subcounty framework for local government in North West Connemara*. Forum, undated, 3 pp.

Anne O'Mahony: *Transport provision in rural areas - proposal to the Departments of Transport, Tourism and Communications, Environment, Social Welfare and Health*. Forum, undated, 16 pp.

Marieke Lientvaar: *A socio-economic profile and plan for Inishbofin*. Forum, September 1992, 38 pp.

Conference and seminar papers

Forum: *Presentation to Poverty 3 seminar on evaluation, 19/20 November 1992*. Forum, undated, 6 pp.

Forum: *The health and social effects of unemployment*. Paper presented to the Cooperation North conference in Dundalk, November 1992, 8 pp.

John Kevaney: *Who is responsible for care in the Community?* Paper by Forum to the conference on the future of community health care in Ireland organized by the Mid-Western Health Board, Co Clare. Forum, November 1992, 9 pp.

Unpublished papers
Chris Curtin: *Forum discussion document.* Forum, January 1991, 9 pp.

Anne Byrne: *Interim report on the progress of the baseline study of poverty in north-west Connemara.* Forum, 1991, 6 pp.

Chris Curtin: *Impact evaluation in the Forum project.* Forum, November 1992.

Cormorant Telematic Systems: *Job creation and north and west Connemara through telework - a report on its potential to Forum.* November 1992, 33 pp.

Forum: *Youth and education.* Forum, undated, 6 pp.

Forum: *Elderly section.* Forum, undated, 6 pp.

Forum: *Primary health care proposal for north west Connemara - work preview, July/December 1992.* Forum, undated, 4 pp.

Chris Curtin: *Discussion document on Forum - the first five months.* Forum, undated, 10 pp.

Kathleen Fahy: *North west Connemara visitor survey - June August 1991.* Forum, 1991. University College Galway, 36 pp.

Patrick Commins, Ena Coleman & Patrick Keogh: *Economic integration through marine resources utilization: State agency, local enterprise and model action partnership in fish farming development in Ireland.* Dublin, Research and Development Unit, May 1993, 8 pp.

Janet O'Toole: *Adult education - Spring 1993 - report on questionnaire.* Forum, July 1993.

Mary Syron & Yvonne Keane: *A study of the informal carers in the Ballyconneely area.* Forum, July 1993, 50 pp.

Catherine Forde: *Evaluation of the Forum enterprise and community development course.* Unpublished, undated (probably 1993), 13 pp.

Forum: *Report on the information day and feedback from the workshop groups held by Ballyconneely community health committee, Ballyconneely, 12 July 1993.* Forum, 1993.

Mary Ruddy: *Community radio and local development.* June 1993.

Progress and planning reports
Proposal. Forum, 1989, 48 pp.

First progress report, March 1989-September 1990. Forum, 1990.

Report for the 2nd contractual period. Forum, undated, 16 pp.

Report for the 3rd contractual period, June 1991 to June 1992. Forum, 1992, 88 pp.

Interim activity and financial report for the 3rd phase to 31 December 1991. 14pp.

Interim activity and financial report for the 3rd phase to 31 December 1991.

Activity and financial report for the 4th contractual phase to 30 June 1993. Forum, 1993, 18 pp.

The delivery of health care service in north and west Connemara. Forum, June 1992.

Summary of main activities. Forum, undated, 6 pp.

Plan of work, 1992-94. Forum, undated, 24 pp.

Newsletters
Forum News. Issues 1 - 5

Material published elsewhere
Margaret McCarthy: 'Planning for north west Connemara'. *Poverty Today.* Issue 13. March 1991.

Jenny O'Reilly & Chris Curtin: 'Getting there is north west Connemara'. *Poverty Today.* Issue 16. January 1992.

Catriona Nic Giolla Phadraig: 'Working with women in Connemara'. *Poverty Today.* Issue 17, April 1992.

Mary Ruddy: 'Who benefits from tourism?' *Poverty Today.* Issue 21 Apr/June 1993.

Mary Ruddy: 'Primary health care project'. *Poverty Today.* Issue 23. Oct/Dec 1993.

Padraig Yeates: 'When a patient's charter does not give access to health care'. *Irish Times,* 8 September 1992, p 10.

Anne Byrne: 'Working for the health of rural women' in Cecily Kelleher (Ed): *The future for health promotion.* Centre for health promotion studies, University College Galway, undated, pp.77-97

PAUL

Published reports
Mary O'Donoghue: *Educational costs and welfare provision for low-income families.* Research report No. 1. PAUL, 1991, 76 pp.

Tom Ronayne & Eoin Devereux: *Labour market provision for the long-term unemployed: the Social Employment Scheme.* Research report No. 2 PAUL, March 1992, 55 pp.

Mary O'Donoghue: _Moving forward together: a study of community needs in Our Lady of Lourdes parish._ PAUL/OLLCSG, Sept. 1993.

Stuart Stamp: _A money advice handbook for advisers in the Republic of Ireland._ PAUL May 1993, 54 pp.

PAUL: _Turning the tide of unemployment._ Leaflet, 8 pp, Undated.

PAUL: _1994 - The road ahead._ 20 pp,. Undated.

Jim Walsh (Ed): _Directory of services in Limerick City:_ PAUL, Citizens Information Centre, Junior Chamber & Limerick Social Services, Sept. 1993, 139 pp.

Submissions and policy documents
PAUL: _Toward an inclusive education service - submission on green paper Education for a changing world._ PAUL, April 1993, 25 pp.

PAUL: _Proposal for a pilot project to tackle indebtedness and to develop credit options for low-income families in Limerick city._ (Submitted to the Department of Social Welfare). PAUL, 12 June 1993, 15 pp.

PAUL: _Proposal for the development of an adult guidance service in Limerick city._ PAUL, undated, 14 pp.

PAUL: _Toward a participative housing management policy - submission by the PAUL partnership on the Memorandum on the preparation of a statement of policy on housing management._ PAUL, undated, 12 pp.

PAUL: _Proposal on policy and strategies post-1993 structural funds and the new cohesion funds._ 3 pp, undated.

PAUL: _Submission on the Consumer Credit Bill._ PAUL, June 1993.

Conference and seminar papers
PAUL: _Key points from presentation to Partners in development conference, Dun Laoghaire, 19/21 February 1991._ PAUL, undated, 9 pp.

Unpublished papers
NEXUS: _PAUL project Limerick - internal evaluation report, final report._ NEXUS, Dublin, December 1990, 99 pp.

Mary E Mulcahy, Cathal O'Connell & Denis Staunton: _Meeting the needs of young people in Moyross - toward effective interventions - a research report commissioned for the PAUL partnership._ Social Policy Research Unit, University College Cork, February 1993, 77 pp.

John Hanna: _Report to PAUL education committee on the early school leaver._ PAUL, first draft, 1993, 25 pp.

References and bibliography

Progress and planning reports
Final report on the definition phase. PAUL, 12 October 1990.

Strategic work plan 1991-94. PAUL, 23 July 91, 25 pp.

Progress report, November 1991. 12 pp.

Progress report No. 3, July 1991-June. 1992.

Progress report, November 1992. 14pp.

Final report, phase 2, October 1990-June 1991. 20 pp.

Draft report, phase 3. July 1991 - June 1992. 55 pp.

Project overview, 26 August 1992. 28 pp.

Newsletters
PAUL News. Issues 1 - 4

Material published elsewhere
'PAUL project profile' *Poverty Today.* Issue 14. June 1991.

Forthcoming
Carmel Duggan and Majella Cosgrove: *Participation costs on labour market programmes for the long-term unemployed.* PAUL, April 1994.

Kenneth Shanks: *The debt crisis: a low income perspective.* PAUL, May 1994.

Dublin Travellers Education and Development Group

Published reports and books
Derek Speirs: *Pavee pictures.* Pavee Point Publications, 1991, 44 pp, £9.99.

John O'Connell: *Ethnicity and Irish Travellers.* DTEDG, October 1991.

Irish Travellers Movement: *No place to go - Travellers accommodation: report on a crisis situation.* DTEDG and Irish Travellers Movement, Pavee Point Publications, 1992, 16 pp.

DTEDG, ICCL & ITM: *Anti-racist laws and the Travellers.* DTEDG and Irish Council for Civil Liberties, 1993, 72 pp, £5.

DTEDG: *Irish Travellers - new analysis and initiatives.* Pavee Point Publications, 1992, 108 pp.

DTEDG: *Traveller words, Traveller ways.* Pavee Point Publications, undated, 205 pp.

ITM: *Travellers and Education.* DTEDG and Irish Travellers Movement, 1993, 34pp.

DTEDG: *President Robinson awards for the design of Traveller accommodation.* Pavee Point Publications, 1993, 36 pp.

DTEDG: *Travellers' accommodation.* Pavee Point Productions, 1993. 36 pp.

DTEDG: *Are you scheming? A guide for Traveller groups.* 1993. 48 pp.

Submissions and policy documents
DTEDG: *Submission on the needs of Traveller children at post-primary level schooling.* DTEDG, May 1991, 12 pp.

DTEDG: *Area-based response to long-term unemployment under the Programme for Economic and Social Progress - notes on the inclusion of Travellers.* DTEDG, July 1991, 4 pp.

DTEDG: *Comment on aspects relating to Gypsies and Travellers in the first annual report of the European Communities' observatory on national policies to combat social exclusion.* DTEDG, July 1991, 3 pp.

DTEDG: *Response to the Programme for Government.* DTEDG, January 1993, 5 pp.

Brona Tennyson: *Recycling and the Traveller economy - income, jobs and wealth creation.* Pavee Point Publications, 1993; research by Environmental Management and Auditing Service Ltd. 55pp.

DTEDG: *Equal status legislation in non-employment areas.* DTEDG, September 1993. 8pp.

Submission to the European Commission on the green paper on social policy. DTEDG, June 1993.

DTEDG: Submission to Department of Health in relation to national health strategy. DTEDG, September 1993, 26pp.

Conference and seminar papers
John O'Connell (Ed): *Report on the EC Gypsy/Traveller education seminar held in Bellinter conference centre, Navan, Co. Meath from 1-4 July 1993.* DTEDG/ITM, July 1993, 20 pp.

Progress and planning reports
Application for funding for a community development project with travelling people. DTEDG, July 1987, 5 pp.

Strategic Plan, 1991-94. DTEDG, 1991, 28 pp.

Report for 1st contractual period, March 1990 to September 1990.

Interim report to Poverty 3. DTEDG, July 1992.

Programme for 3rd contractual period, July 1991 to June 1992. 6 pp.

Programme for 4th contractual period, July 1992 to June 1993. 10 pp.

Poverty 3 innovatory initiative. DTEDG, undated, 4 pp.

Newsletters
Traveller Economy. Issues 1 - 5

Eurofocus. Issues 1 - 4.

Other publications
'Travellers at school'. Education & living, *Irish Times*, 23 November 1993.

Padraig Yeates: 'Travellers generate up to 400 jobs'. *Irish Times.* 29 October 1993.

Paul O'Kane: 'Who are the travellers? How many are there?' *Irish Times.* 23 November 1993.

Task force on the travelling community, education and training subcommittee: Report and recommendations. January 1994.

Michael Smith: *Address at the opening exhibition of the entries for the President Robinson awards for the design of traveller accommodation.* Dublin, Department of the Environment, 4 February 1993, 4 pp.

Ireland

June Meehan: 'Third European anti-poverty programme'. *Poverty Today.* Issue No. 9. March 1990.

Seamus O Cinneide with Carmel Corrigan: *Social exclusion in Ireland - part I of the second annual report for Ireland for the EC observatory on national policies to combat social exclusion.* St Patrick's College, Maynooth, Co Kildare, June 1992, 153 pp.

Kieran McKeown: *Poverty 3 - European Community Programme to foster economic and social integration: an analytical overview.* Combat Poverty Agency, April 1993, 36pp.

Seamus O Cinneide: *Evaluating Poverty 3 at the national level - a discussion paper presented to the S'Agaro workshop.* July 1991, 9 pp.

Patrick Commins: *Meeting the challenges of exclusion and underdevelopment in rural areas: the role of tourism:* A&R, May 1992. 20pp.

Patrick Commins (Ed): *Combating exclusion in Ireland, 1990-94, a midway report.* Combat Poverty Agency, March 1993, 42 pp.

A&R: *Report on 1st seminar of EC Poverty 3 programme on conference held in Furbo, Co Galway, July 1990.* Lille, France, undated, 19 pp.

A&R: *Report of the Research and Development Unit Ireland for the third contractual period, 1 November 1991 to 30 June 1992.* Lille, France, undated, 62 pp.

Mary Daly: *Discussion document - evaluation of the model action projects in the third EC anti-poverty programme.* Combat Poverty Agency, undated, 9 pp.

Mary Daly: *Women and poverty.* Dublin, Attic press, 1989, 142 pp.

Margaret Barry: *Participation - an issue in the European Poverty Programme. Participation seminar, Netherlands, June 1992.* Combat Poverty Agency, 8 pp.

Seamus O Cinneide: *Scheme for recording data relating to projects.* A&R, Lille, June 1990, 16 pp.

Frank Gaffikin & Mike Morrissey: *Planning for partnership in the third EC programme - the role of evaluation.* Unpublished, paper, November 1992, 22 pp.

Bernadette Barry: *Lofty ideals, tangible results - interim report by the projects in the Republic of Ireland in the second European programme to Combat Poverty.* Dublin, Combat Poverty Agency, 1988.

Barry Cullen: *Poverty, community and development - a report on the issues of social policy that have arisen in the work of the nine projects of the second European programme to combat poverty, 1985-89.* Dublin, Combat Poverty Agency, 1989.

Hugh Frazer: *Integrated rural development - a solution to rural poverty.* Joint north/south conference organized by the Combat Poverty Agency and the Rural Action Project, Galway, 8-9 April 1988.

Brian Nolan & Brian Farrell: *Child poverty in Ireland.* Dublin, Combat Poverty Agency, 1990, 113 pp.

Europe

Graham Room et al: *Observatory on national policies to combat social exclusion, second annual report.* Commission of the European Communities, 1993, 136 pp + app.

Graham Room: *Anti-poverty action-research in Europe.* Bristol, School for Advanced Urban Studies, 1993.

Commission of the European Communities: *Final report on the second European anti-poverty programme, 1985-89.* Brussels. Ref: COM 91/29 final, 13 February 1991.

Commission of the European Communities: *Medium-term action programme to foster the economic and social integration of the least privileged groups.* Bulletin of the European Communities, Supplement 4/89. Brussels, 1989.